Western Branch Lines

DAVID SOGGEE & MICHAEL WELCH

Capital Transport

ISBN 978-1-85414-349-5

Published by
Capital Transport Publishing
www.capitaltransport.com

Printed by
1010 Printing International Ltd

© Michael Welch 2011

Front cover: The shadows are lengthening as a train waits in Bampton station's southbound platform prior to departure to Exeter on 13th October 1962. There were two 'Bamptons' on the Western Region and, in order to avoid confusion with a station on the Oxford to Fairford branch, this station was described as 'Bampton (Devon)' in the public timetable. One wonders whether the station in Oxfordshire was as picturesque as that seen here. Note the signal, high on the side of the cutting, beyond the overbridge.

Back cover: A lost 'Inter City' route? In the 1960s BR developed the 'Inter City' brand for their main-line express services, but not all routes connecting cities were considered worthy of development, an example being the line that linked the moderately-sized county 'towns' (actually cities) of Gloucester and Hereford. This single-track route served few intermediate places of any importance and was closed from 2nd November 1964. Here, in this shot taken on 19th September 1964, a Gloucester-bound train is about to plunge into the depths of Ballingham tunnel.

Title page: For much of the 1950s the regular Fowey branch engine was 0-4-2T No.1419 which is depicted here in charge of a branch train near Lostwithiel, on 16th May 1959. In that year it was the only locomotive of its class allocated to St Blazey shed. The summer 1961 timetable advertised eight trains on Mondays to Fridays along the 5½ miles-long branch, with eleven services being provided on Saturdays.

Introduction

David Soggee cannot remember how he first became interested in railways – there was certainly no railway background in his family. In the mid-1940s his local station was Manor Park, on the former Great Eastern Railway (GER) main line from Liverpool Street to Norwich, and he recalls seeing LNER 4-6-0s such as No. 2870 *City of London* and 8302 *Eland* in addition to an assortment of tank locomotives employed on suburban duties. In about 1946 he ventured across London to Paddington station and travelled from Westbourne Park station to Old Oak Lane Halt on a push-pull train. David is unsure of the precise date but it must have been before 30th June because the latter station closed on that date!

By this time his passion for trains was well established and it was perhaps inevitable that he opted to work on BR, joining as an apprentice fitter and turner at Stratford works in 1949. During this time he worked on all the GER classes, plus LNER types and BR Standard Class 4MT 2-6-0s, all of which visited the works for a heavy overhaul, so he can claim to have really 'got his hands dirty' working on steam traction. This experience of working with steam did not dampen his enthusiasm, much of his leisure time being spent touring the railway system, and he developed a particular affection for the branch line scene, both in Great Britain and Ireland, and David reckons he took his first black and white railway photograph way back in 1951. He started colour photography in 1958 and experimented with various makes before deciding that Kodachrome film was far superior to other brands and he became a loyal Kodak customer despite the fact that the film was extremely expensive, costing thirty-five shillings (£1.75) for a 36-exposure roll. He says even his 50 year-old transparencies have shown very little deterioration over the years, so the massive financial outlay, which was keenly felt at the time, was more than justified. During the last ten years of BR steam traction David amassed around 230 films but this figure also includes shots taken in Ireland and during visits to mainland Europe, where he took a special interest in narrow gauge lines. He used an Agfa Silette camera which served him well for a long period until it was replaced by an Asahi Pentax S1 in 1969. David may have spent a lot on film, but this was balanced by the fact that as a BR employee he was entitled to extensive free and reduced rate travel which enabled him to rove far and wide across Great Britain, recording the branch line scene before it was swept away forever by the infamous Beeching axe of the 1960s. It was very much a race against time and, in addition to regular weekend expeditions, very often entire summer holidays would be spent in search of steam, with Ireland – where the railway scene had an irresistible charm all of its own – being a regular destination.

One of his favourite BR regions was without question the 'Western' and the very wide variety of views in this album bear testament to the numerous journeys he made to visit sometimes obscure branch lines before they succumbed to closure. One of the first closures of a WR branch he witnessed was in February 1953 when the little-known Blaengarw to Brynmenyn line lost its passenger service. He especially liked the Watlington branch, which ran from Princes Risborough along the edge of the Chiltern Hills via Aston Rowfant and Chinnor, but this route closed on 1st July 1957, twelve months before David took up colour photography, so he has only pictures taken in black and white. Another of the WR branch lines for which he had a special affection was the idyllic Exe Valley line that ran from Exeter St Davids to Dulverton via Tiverton, and David was able to photograph steam trains in colour on the line prior to its sad closure in October 1963. He was a great fan of the GWR Class 4500/4575 2-6-2 tank locomotives and he enjoyed travelling over many of the Cornish branches behind those classes, which were an integral part of many WR branch line operations.

Compilation of this album has benefited from assistance given by Chris Evans, Dave Fakes, John Langford and Graham Mallinson who have kindly read through the text and suggested many alterations and improvements which have undoubtedly enhanced the final product and grateful thanks are due to these gentlemen. The tickets and luggage labels were provided by Les Dench and David Soggee. Design and typesetting by Lucy Frontani and Kate McKellar.

Michael Welch
Burgess Hill, West Sussex
August 2011

Contents

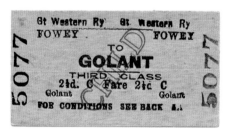

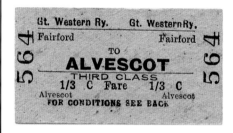

The branch line from Maidenhead to Marlow was opened in stages and constructed by two separate companies. The section from Maidenhead to Marlow Road (later Bourne End) was built by the Wycombe Railway Company as part of the route connecting Maidenhead with High Wycombe. This company obtained its Act of Parliament in July 1846 and construction started in 1852, the line being opened throughout on 1st August 1854. The Wycombe Railway Company was taken over by the GWR on 1st February 1867. In August 1867 the businessmen of Great Marlow met to discuss the possibilities of a link with this line at Marlow Road station and the result was the Great Marlow Railway Act which was given the Royal Assent on 13th July 1868 with an authorised share capital of £18,000. One third of this sum was raised locally, the balance being supplied by the GWR. The 2¾ miles-long line from Marlow Road to Marlow was opened on 27th June 1873, the former station being renamed Bourne End in 1874 to avoid confusion. The local company maintained the line and provided the staff, but the GWR supplied and operated the rolling stock, motive power normally being a 0-4-2ST locomotive dating from 1868. The GWR acquired the remainder of the capital and took over ownership of the line from 1897. In this view of Maidenhead station taken on 29th June 1961 an up train is seen running in with 'Castle' Class 4-6-0 No.7037 *Swindon* in charge. This locomotive was built at Swindon works (as its name suggests!) and was released to traffic in August 1950. The line through Maidenhead was opened in 1840 and the original station was located east of the river Thames. The station depicted here, originally called Maidenhead Junction, was opened on 1st November 1871. Note the solidly built telephone booth which gave users a considerable degree of privacy.

THE MARLOW BRANCH

A portrait of Bourne End station taken on 20th September 1958 showing the Marlow auto-train waiting in the bay platform. Note that the level crossing gates at the far end of the station are open so presumably a train to or from High Wycombe was expected. The lines from Maidenhead and Marlow converged just behind the photographer, the route from the former crossing the river Thames on a bridge in order to enter the station while the Marlow line ran along the north bank of the river.

A number of trains from Maidenhead terminated at Bourne End while those to High Wycombe paused in the platform for six or seven minutes, so one can only speculate regarding the identity of this train headed by a GWR 6100 Class 2-6-2T locomotive in black livery. This shot was taken from the footbridge seen in the previous picture and shows the line towards High Wycombe. Note the signal box and the token apparatus for the single line section. In the summer 1961 timetable there were around ten weekday trains between Maidenhead, Bourne End and High Wycombe, some of which were through workings from Paddington; there was a token service of two trains each way on Sundays. The service was noteworthy for the very long six-hour gap in the middle of the day on Mondays to Fridays. The line from Bourne End to High Wycombe was closed to passenger traffic from 4th May 1970 but, perhaps, the station fruiterers, on the right, still remains in business! This picture was taken on 28th May 1960.

The Marlow branch was famous for its mixed trains and in this shot 1400 Class 0-4-2T No.1421, in quite clean condition, is seen just after leaving Marlow on a sunny 29th June 1961. At the time of this photograph four of these locomotives were based in the London area, this particular example being allocated to Reading shed, while others were based at Slough and Southall.

A scene at Marlow engine shed also on 29th June 1961. Railway aficionados may have great affection for the 'great and glorious' days of steam but for many of those involved in the day to day operation of the railway using steam traction 'dirty, dangerous and laborious' is probably the description they would prefer. Even a small branch-line engine needs to have clinker removed from its firebox and in this shot No.1421's fireman is obviously busy on the footplate cleaning the fire. At least his activities have produced an interesting and unusual picture for the photographer, who timed his exposure just right! The small, smoke-blackened shed seen here was a sub-shed of Slough for many years.

An absolutely charming branch line scene. The train has been marshalled, the engine has just been coupled up and the crew await the 'right away' for the short trip to Bourne End on 29th June 1961. Note the barrow (complete with luggage!) and the elaborate platform lamps which seem to be a bit on the large side for such a small station. For many years the service has been affectionately known to the local people as the 'Marlow Donkey', a name which is believed to have originated from the trains of pack horses, mules and donkeys that were used to carry goods to the riverside for onward transportation. Sadly, the steam-hauled 'Marlow Donkey' ran for the last time on Sunday 8th July 1962 when steam was ousted by a more economical diesel unit.

A dull winter's day – 14th January 1961. Parliamentary authorisation for the extension of the Wycombe Railway from Princes Risborough to Oxford was obtained on 28th June 1861. Construction was rapid and a service from Thame to Paddington via Maidenhead commenced on 1st August 1862. Traffic on the line was in decline by the early 1930s which prompted the GWR to introduce rail-motors as an economy measure and a new halt was opened in 1933 at Towersey, between Princes Risborough and Thame, to encourage more people to use the line. In the winter 1954/55 timetable a paltry service of around half a dozen weekday trains was advertised with two on Sundays. The end came for passenger trains on the line on 7th January 1963 with BR claiming an annual saving of £34,372. In this picture GWR 2-6-2T No.6163 is seen taking water at Thame while working an eastbound train towards Princes Risborough; sister engine No.6154 stands on the right with a goods working.

A snowy January day in 1963. The level of snow is up to the top of the rails in this photograph of 2-6-2T No.6111 taking water at Thame whilst powering a train to Princes Risborough. The station's fine overall roof will be noted. Regrettably, services were withdrawn from this route shortly after this picture was taken, a surprising decision in view of the line's close proximity to London and potential use as a diversionary route.

Ambitions unrealised. The Wallingford & Watlington Railway Act of July 1864 authorised the construction of the 2¾ miles-long line from Cholsey to Wallingford and it was planned to extend the line six miles to Watlington, but this idea was stifled by lack of finance, the plan being abandoned in December 1868. Construction of the line to Wallingford was straightforward because there were no intermediate stations nor engineering works of any size and the branch opened on 2nd July 1866. The line was worked by the GWR from the outset and that company took over completely on 2nd December 1872 after the local company got into financial trouble. There was a small, plain terminal station building at Wallingford, a locomotive shed that was a sub depot of Didcot, and a goods yard consisting of four sidings, one of which served a goods shed. Most importantly, there was a gasworks and a creamery, both of which brought goods traffic to the branch.

A very intensive passenger service was operated and in 1937 this consisted of eighteen return trips on weekdays, so this was no sleepy branch line! There were, however, no trains on Sundays. By the mid-1950s the service had declined somewhat, only eleven return trains being advertised, and the line was closed to passengers from 15th June 1959 but Wallingford station remained open for goods until 13th September 1965. A stub continued to serve an industrial installation until 1981 and the end of this service was commemorated when BR ran a special train on 31st May 1981. A society was subsequently formed to preserve a section of the line. In this photograph 1400 Class 0-4-2T No.1444, which worked the branch for many years, is seen powering an auto-coach on 13th June 1959, the last day of BR passenger services. On 21st September 1968 steam traction made a comeback on the branch when preserved 1400 Class No.1466, which was based at nearby Didcot, worked auto trains on the branch in contravention of the infamous BR ban on steam traction then in force.

Photographed on a dreary day, 11th April 1959, Wallingford station and 1400 Class 0-4-2T No.1444 plus its auto-coach presented rather a drab and uninspiring scene, the only colourful item being a poster extolling the virtues of Nine Elms paints, a brand name with 'Southern' connections. The engine shed, which is partially visible on the left, was built by the GWR around the turn of the century and was constructed of red brick under a slate roof. In the background, beyond the buffer stops, part of the station master's house can be seen. The water supply for the conical-topped water tank came from a well situated immediately behind the station platform; for many years the pump was powered by a small steam engine until it was replaced by an electric motor.

The 2½ miles-long branch line from Radley to Abingdon, which was originally broad gauge, was constructed by the Abingdon Railway and opened on 2nd June 1856; it was operated by the GWR from the outset. It is recorded that the land upon which Abingdon station was built cost £472, and seven properties, including a public house, had to be demolished to make way for the station. A replacement pub was later built at a different location. The Abingdon Railway was absorbed by the GWR on 15th August 1904. The winter 1954/55 timetable reveals that on weekdays the service was quite lavish, with sixteen trains each way being provided, and the timetable states that between 2.00pm and 4.30pm passengers were able to travel on the City of Oxford Motor Services' buses because no train service was available during that time. There were three trains each way on Sundays, all of which ran during the afternoon. Latterly former GWR 0-4-2Ts worked the passenger service until diesel railcars took over and for many years they were the only steam locomotives allowed on the line. The branch was closed to passenger traffic on 8th September 1963 but goods traffic, particularly MG cars from a local factory, remained relatively buoyant and this was worked by pannier tank engines that had been given special clearance to work over the line in 1962. The last goods trains ran in the mid-1980s. In this picture a BR single-unit railcar is seen waiting to leave Abingdon on 18th May 1963. Note the rather 'lonely' running-in board and splendidly ornate gas lamp standard.

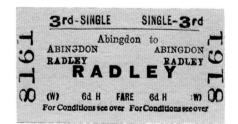

Opened by the Lambourn Valley Railway (LVR) on 4th April 1898, the 12½ miles-long branch from Newbury to Lambourn was a late arrival on the scene and was destined to have a short life of just over sixty years. The line originally had no fewer than seven stations, two of which were later downgraded to the status of halts. Remarkably, in the very early years the LVR possessed a fleet of three steam locomotives, four coaches and several goods wagons, the last-mentioned being second-hand purchases, and for a short period the LVR hired two rail-motors from the GWR. On 1st July 1905 the GWR assumed control of the line and almost immediately replaced the line's motley collection of rolling stock with standard GWR locomotives and coaches. The branch then led a sleepy existence for many years, the winter 1954/55 timetable indicating a service of six return, third class only trains each weekday; there were no trains on Sundays. A noteworthy development was the construction of a branch to a United States Air Force base at Welford Park. The line traversed a thinly populated area and the passenger service was withdrawn from 4th January 1960, the last trains running on Saturday 2nd January, so it was hardly a 'Happy New Year' for the line's regular customers. Former GWR 2251 Class 0-6-0 No.3210 is seen running into Speen station with an afternoon Lambourn-bound train on 22nd August 1959.

Subsidence, mostly due to colliery workings under railway lines, was a major problem in some areas but is extremely unlikely to have caused the waiting shelter at East Garston station to develop such a pronounced lean. Perhaps the local rabbit population had something to answer for! Anyway, the train depicted here seems to be assured of picking up at least one passenger. The locomotive hauling this one-coach train to Lambourn is a rather grimy pannier tank locomotive No.4665 and this picture was also taken on 22nd August 1959. Note the wagon in the goods siding.

No.3210 is seen again, this time posing at Lambourn station on the same date as the two previous photographs. This locomotive hauled the 4.12pm from Newbury to Lambourn on the last day, Saturday 2nd January 1960, and also the 5.15pm empty stock train back to Newbury on which passengers were permitted to travel. These trains were composed of two GWR compartment coaches. The last passenger train from Newbury to Lambourn was powered by 0-6-0 No.2212 and consisted of five GWR compartment carriages, a LMSR luggage van and, rather appropriately bearing in mind Lambourn's connections with the horse racing world, a horse box. The very last passenger train of all to traverse the full length of the branch was the 6.05pm from Lambourn which eventually left exactly an hour late, apparently due to people pulling the communication cord, and Newbury was reached 1½ hours late. The line north of Welford Park was closed completely but the section south thereof lasted until November 1973 to serve the air force base, and on 3rd November a farewell special ran up and down the line to give the public the opportunity of a final trip over what remained of this little-known backwater.

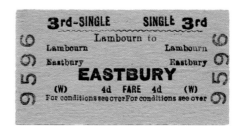

(4237)

BRITISH RLYS. (Western Region)

TO

LAMBOURN

3rd-SINGLE   SINGLE 3rd

Lambourn to

Lambourn   Lambourn

9596   Eastbury   Eastbury   9596

EASTBURY

(W)   4d FARE 4d   (W)

For conditions see over For conditions see over

A picture of Savernake (Low Level) station taken on 19th August 1961, looking westwards towards Pewsey, with the Marlborough branch junction visible in the background. The station here was opened by the Berkshire & Hampshire Extension Railway (BHER) on 11th November 1862, when it commenced operation of its broad gauge link from Hungerford to Devizes. Originally, the station consisted of only one platform, on the up side, but there was a crossing loop which meant that if trains wished to cross each other, one had to shunt into the loop. The station building, located in beautiful surroundings, had twin gables and for many years boasted a refreshment room. The 5½ miles-long branch line to Marlborough was proposed by the Marlborough Railway Company and opened on 14th April 1864. The BHER line was converted to standard gauge in 1874 and the BHER was purchased by the GWR on 1st July 1882. In 1873 the Swindon, Marlborough & Andover Railway (SMAR) obtained an Act to build two sections of line, one from Swindon to Marlborough, and another from Wolfhall Junction, just east of Savernake, to a spot near Andover Junction. The SMAR, which later became part of the Midland & South Western Junction Railway (MSWJR), had been granted running powers over the Marlborough to Savernake section; the GWR was very hostile to this scheme but was forced to allow the SMAR's trains to pass through. Even worse for the GWR, a Board of Trade inspector surveying the line of the SMAR insisted that Savernake station needed drastic improvements in order to accommodate the traffic of both the SMAR and the GWR, and the latter was forced to construct a down platform, new footbridge, additional sidings and signal boxes at each end of the station, this work being finished in about 1883. The GWR continued to be as obstructive as possible to the interloper, which it regarded as a potential competitor, and eventually the MSWJR decided to build its own independent route, avoiding the GWR's Savernake station, between Marlborough and a spot east of Savernake (later Grafton South Junction) where it connected with its Andover line. This involved building a separate high-level station at Savernake, which opened on 26th June 1898. History repeated itself when, on 15th September 1958, Savernake (High Level) station was closed and trains on the MSWJR diverted to run via the low level station once again but, presumably, without the acrimony of previous times. Passenger trains on the MSWJR ceased to run from 11th September 1961 while the low level station, seen here, lasted until 18th April 1966. It should be noted that goods traffic continued on some sections well after the line closed to passengers and the stretch from Andover to Ludgershall is still operational at the time of writing.

In 1845 the Bristol & Exeter Railway (B&ER) was authorised by an Act of Parliament to construct a broad gauge, single track line from Taunton to Yeovil, a distance of just over 25 miles. The line ran initially from Durston Junction, on the Taunton to Bristol main line, to Hendford, on the outskirts of Yeovil, and was opened in October 1853, the long delay being attributed to the B&ER giving priority to other schemes. An extension to Yeovil (Pen Mill) station was later completed so the line from Taunton, which was converted to standard gauge in 1879, could link up with a separate route from Frome. Like so many rural lines serving a sparsely populated area, traffic on the route was eroded by the growth in road transport and the inevitable closure took place on 15th June 1964, goods traffic continuing at the Yeovil end until 1968. Interestingly, most branch trains used the original route right up until closure, which involved travelling along the Bristol line from Taunton as far as Durston Junction where they diverged. They joined the main Taunton to Castle Cary line at Athelney Junction and ran along this line, which was built as part of the GWR's 'new direct route to the west' and opened in 1906, as far as Curry Rivell Junction where branch trains turned in a south-easterly direction towards Yeovil. The railway authorities cannot be accused of failing to develop custom on the branch, because halts were opened at various times to tap new sources of traffic, including one at Lyng, between Durston and Athelney, which opened on 24th September 1928. This halt is seen on a dull 30th May 1964 with an anonymous GWR 2-6-2T powering a train towards Yeovil. It would appear that the bridge was built to be able to span a double-track formation.

The train seen in the previous photograph is seen pausing at the intermediate station of Martock. There was a passing loop here to enable trains to cross on the single line, and Martock station was of interest due to its staggered platforms. Towards the end, a service of six trains in each direction was provided on weekdays only. Note the 'Southern' signal which looks out of place on a former GWR branch. This was no doubt a legacy of the short period in the 1950s when the line was under Southern Region control.

Like the line from Taunton to Yeovil, the branch to Chard was also a truly rural line that served few intermediate centres of population but, unlike the Yeovil line, it was initially promoted by a local company, the Chard & Taunton Railway, which obtained an Act of Parliament in 1861. The B&ER soon took control, however, and commenced work on building the route during the following year, the broad gauge line opening to Chard in September 1866. The London & South Western Railway (L&SWR) had opened a separate Chard Town station three years earlier and on 26th November 1866 a spur was opened to connect the town's two stations, but through running was not possible until the line from Taunton was converted to standard gauge in 1891. The L&SWR subsequently closed Chard Town station and all services were concentrated on the B&ER's premises which were known as Chard Joint (renamed Chard Central in 1949). The branch was closed temporarily due to a fuel crisis in 1951, but traffic was being steadily eroded by the growth in private motoring and permanent closure to passenger traffic occurred on 10th September 1962. In this shot, taken on 29th July 1961, a train bound for Chard hauled by 8750 Class pannier tank locomotive No.4663 runs into the modest station of Hatch, which was built in the Brunel-style. This station formerly possessed a goods loop but only one platform so it was not possible to cross passenger trains there. Note the 154 yards-long Hatch tunnel in the background. Perhaps the young children on the platform were about to go for their first ride on the line.

Three gentlemen engaged in quiet conversation at Ilminster station as pannier tank engine No.4663 simmers in the platform with the train seen in the previous photograph. The people on the platform are likely to be the train's guard and, perhaps, the station booking clerk while the person in the locomotive's cab is presumably the driver or fireman. This station has the usual equipment, gas lighting, an ancient platform barrow and a seat that was probably as old as the station itself. Note the religious poster stating that the 'Holy scriptures are able to make thee wise until salvation'.

In this picture, which was also taken on 29th July 1961, No.4663 is seen steaming off into the distance bound for Chard, while the branch goods, with a 5700 Class pannier tank engine in charge, waits patiently by the signal box. This picture shows part of the station building, this being the original, very attractive Bristol & Exeter Railway station. Ilminster only had one platform and although there was a passing loop it was not signalled for use by passenger trains, therefore it was not possible for two passenger trains to pass there. The signal box remained in occasional use until the line north of Chard was closed completely in 1964. No.4663 was based at Taunton for many years and seems to have been a regular performer on the line; it had the dubious privilege of hauling the very last passenger train to leave Ilminster, this being the 9.30pm Chard Central to Taunton on 8th September 1962.

A shot of the north end of Chard Central station, taken on the same day as the previous three pictures, which nicely captures the branch's unhurried atmosphere. Class 5700 0-6-0PT engine No.5779 stands on the left in the bay platform with (what appears to be) a former slip coach that was being used at about this time on the shuttle service to and from Chard Junction station, on the 'Southern's Salisbury to Exeter line. The locomotive on the right is presumably waiting to leave with a train bound for Taunton. The summer 1962 passenger timetable advertised a very sparse service of only five weekday trains in each direction between Taunton and Chard, one of which was an 'express' and left Taunton at the ungodly hour of 6.00am: perhaps it carried newspaper traffic. This train was booked to call only at Ilminster and was scheduled to cover the 15¼ miles in exactly an hour. The service from Chard to Chard Junction was a little better with eight weekday trains. There was no service at all along the entire length of the line on Sundays. The lines north and south of Chard Central were largely operated as two separate routes, trains being timed to make connections for Chard at Taunton and Chard Junction. Due to the very infrequent service, through passengers on the branch really had to be determined and patient travellers because they were faced with long waits at Chard Central, sometimes well in excess of half an hour.

Summer holiday time! After the end of the Second World War, holidays with pay became an established feature of life in Great Britain and this prompted a huge surge in the number of people taking a traditional British seaside holiday. In the 1950s car ownership was the preserve of the better off and the masses travelled by train, generally taking their annual break during the school holiday months of July and August. This mass exodus placed a huge burden on the railway's resources and it sometimes struggled to cope: goods engines were often pressed into service on passenger work. In the Beeching era, the provision of little-used sets of coaching stock to meet the peak summer demand was deemed to be uneconomic and summer holiday trains quickly disappeared from the timetables. One of the most popular destinations for holiday-makers were the Channel Islands, which were reached by ferry from Weymouth, and passengers from the London area usually took one of the many boat trains that ran from Waterloo. In this view of Weymouth quay, taken on 2nd September 1961, all three platforms are occupied by boat trains and the port appears to be working at full capacity. The locomotives in this picture are 8750 Class 0-6-0PT No.9620, on the left, and 1366 Class 0-6-0PT No.1369 on the right.

Confrontation on the streets of Weymouth! For many passengers on boat trains to Weymouth the last leg of the journey on the tramway, along the narrow streets of the town, must have been quite a novelty but for the railway's operating staff it was something of a nightmare at times. Did they receive extra pay for the stress and harassment involved? Ordinary motorists, traders and delivery men had a nasty habit of parking on the railway tracks and in this picture a delivery van belonging to a local firm appears to be blocking the path of No.1369 hauling a boat train set of carriages. Surely the delivery man knew that a train was likely to appear? This picture was also taken on 2nd September 1961. When the Weymouth quay line was authorised by an Act of Parliament in 1862 did its promoters envisage the problems the line would cause in the age of the motor car? When opened in October 1865 it was mixed gauge and worked by horses until about 1884. How quaint!

The prominent running-in board immediately identifies the location of this photograph, which was taken on 27th July 1963. 1400 Class 0-4-2T No.1421 waits to leave the station with a train to Tiverton Junction. This locomotive was an exile from the London area, having been a regular performer on the Marlow branch, and is depicted elsewhere in this album. Note the BR Standard non-corridor suburban coach in the siding; this was presumably held 'spare' and pressed into traffic at busy times. The branch from Tiverton Junction was the first railway to reach Tiverton and opened as a broad gauge line on 12th June 1848. This branch provided the town's only railway link to the outside world for almost a generation, because construction of the Exe Valley routes to Dulverton and Exeter, both of which had been authorised in the mid-1870s, was long-delayed and neither became operational until ten years later. The Tiverton Junction to Tiverton branch was converted to standard gauge in June 1884. For many years Tiverton was reputedly the third largest town in Devon and the station boasted a complement of no fewer than thirty staff. The 4½ miles-long branch was built as a double track route but in the event only one track was laid. By the standards of other Devon branches it was not scenically outstanding but a major point of interest was an aqueduct which carried the Grand Western canal across the track, this being constructed with separate arches for the proposed 'up' and 'down' lines.

TIVERTON TO TIVERTON JUNCTION

Friends in high places. The photographer is a long-standing friend of Fred Pugh, both being members of the GLO group of railway enthusiasts. In 1964 Fred was the stationmaster at Tiverton Junction and in order to give his friends a last chance to photograph steam traction on the Hemyock branch he arranged for steam to be specially rostered, using 1400 Class 0-4-2T No.1450, because the branch had been diesel worked for some time. The special was arranged for 23rd August 1964 but the participants must have been dismayed when they saw that No.1450 was in the deplorable external condition which was so typical of the BR steam fleet at that time. They realised that if they wanted to photograph a reasonably smart engine they would have to clean it themselves, and they immediately embarked on an impromptu cleaning session in an effort to improve No.1450's somewhat blistered paintwork to something approaching a respectable condition and restore its dignity. Prior to journeying along the Hemyock branch No.1450 carried out a little light shunting, and is seen here through the open window of Tiverton Junction signal box marshalling a rake of conflat wagons loaded with FM insulated meat containers which were stabled in the local Lloyd Manners factory's private siding. Or was No.1450 simply playing to the gallery?

When the steep decline in the fortunes of the railway industry occurred after the Second World War, British Railways came under enormous pressure to economise and latterly pursued a 'scorched earth' policy which saw countless station buildings reduced to rubble and rudimentary 'bus stop' shelters provided in their place. Goods yards were ripped up and virtually anything that was perceived to be 'surplus to requirements' was destroyed. This unparalleled orgy of destruction included such things as the huge mechanical concrete coaling plants located at steam locomotive sheds. They were probably the tallest structures of the steam age and could sometimes be seen for miles around; they were very solidly built and explosives usually had to be used to demolish them, often with a large contingent of the local populace looking on. There was nothing quite so massive at Tiverton Junction but this shot at least gives some idea of the infrastructure that existed on the railway system – industrial archaeologists must have had a field day. The principal subject is a water tank (or at least part thereof), painted in regional

colours, with the station footbridge and associated stairway and platform awnings beyond. The water tank probably dated from the Victorian era but the footbridge and its stairways, plus the platform awnings, were presumably installed when the line through Tiverton Junction station was quadrupled, and the station rebuilt, in the 1930s. The premises were closed on 12th May 1986 upon the opening of the nearby Tiverton Parkway station. Almost lost amid the ironwork is a nicely cleaned 1400 Class locomotive, No.1468, which was waiting to proceed down the Hemyock branch, and this photograph was taken on 12th September 1959.

The first station of any consequence down the line from Tiverton Junction (if one disregards Coldharbour Halt) was Uffculme, as pretty a little country railway station as one could wish for. Note the spotless state of the platform and really beautiful floral display. There clearly was no room for the bench on the main part of the platform and, rather strangely, it had been placed on the ramp. The train is probably the 3.00pm from Hemyock and motive power is provided by 0-4-2T No.1468. This picture was also taken on a sunny 12th September 1959. The history of the 7½ miles-long Culm Valley branch can be traced back to 1868 when it became one of the first railways to be sanctioned under the Light Railways Act which became law during that year. The line received the Royal Assent on 15th May 1873 and opened on 29th May 1876, apparently costing £20,000 more to build than had been anticipated; it was taken over by the GWR in April 1880. In view of the very low speeds, passenger traffic was never buoyant and the line's salvation proved to be the Culm Valley Dairy Co. who opened their factory at Hemyock in 1886.

Hauling one passenger coach and a milk tank wagon, No.1468 pauses at Culmstock on 12th September 1959. The carriage is one of a pair of five-compartment former Barry Railway gaslit vehicles (Nos. W263W and W268W) that were the only passenger carriages then passed to work over the branch due to carriage lighting problems. They were replaced by two Thompson-designed coaches (Nos.W87245E and W87270E) in late 1962.

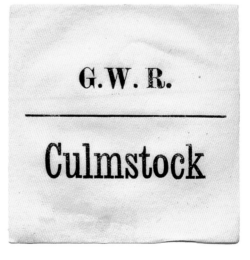

G.W.R.

Culmstock

Thatched cottages across the roadway from the station, a running-in board almost totally hidden by a climbing rosebush, a lovely oil lamp standard and a riot of colourful flowers on the platform. One can almost smell the scent of the roses. This was the scene at Culmstock on the same day that the previous shot was taken. The poster advertising party outings was a trifle inappropriate at Culmstock because customers would presumably have to get back to Tiverton Junction in time for the last train along the branch which, in the summer 1961 timetable, departed at 5.07pm.

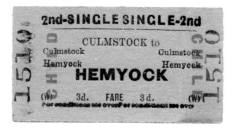

A view of Hemyock showing No.1468 simmering after arrival with the 1.40pm train from Tiverton Junction, this being booked to arrive at 2.20pm. The placid waters of the river Culm are out of sight behind the train. The line followed an extremely sinuous course and ran as close to the meandering river Culm as possible. It was forced around even tighter curves in order to avoid land owned by farmers who opposed its construction and a speed limit of 15mph applied. When the passenger service was withdrawn from 9th September 1963 (the last trains actually ran on Saturday 7th September), little interest was shown by the local people, apart from a fair-sized crowd who turned out to witness the departure of the last service from Hemyock.

The principal source of traffic on the line was from the Culm Valley Dairy Company's factory at Hemyock which, as previously mentioned, opened in 1886. Their premises, which were latterly part of United Dairies Ltd, manufactured cheese, butter and processed milk and it is the last-mentioned commodity by which the line will be especially remembered, due to the regular milk trains that ran to London. In order to maintain fresh supplies these workings ran along the branch seven days a week and it was undoubtedly this profitable traffic that kept the branch in business for so long. The dairy was across the road from the station and in this view a flagman can be seen holding a 'stop' disc while No.1450 undertakes a shunting operation across the road on 23rd August 1964. This was the day when steam had been especially rostered, as previously referred to, so the flagman, and his colleagues in the dairy, probably wondered what on earth was going on! Note the profusion of gates! The dairy closed unexpectedly and after 3rd November 1975 the Culm Valley no longer echoed to the sound of the daily milk train.

Undoubtedly, one of the best-loved branch lines in Devon was the Exe Valley line, which ran 19¼ miles from Stoke Canon, just outside Exeter, to Morebath Junction, on the Taunton to Barnstaple route, from where trains continued 1¾ miles to Dulverton which was just over the county border in Somerset. The line was built in two distinct sections, the route north of Tiverton being promoted by the Tiverton & North Devon Railway, while the stretch south of Tiverton was proposed by the Exe Valley Railway Company. The former company obtained an Act of Parliament in 1875, while the latter was authorised by an Act on 30th June 1874. In the event the line north of Tiverton was the first to open, on 1st August 1884, while the section south thereof was brought into use on 1st May 1885. By this time the broad gauge lines were being converted to standard and the Exe Valley line was built to this gauge from the outset. There were four intermediate crossing points at Thorverton, Cadeleigh, Tiverton and Bampton. The first station after leaving Exeter (if one excludes halts) was at Thorverton and in this photograph an Exeter-bound two-coach auto-train is seen entering on 12th September 1959. A private siding serving a mill was located here and when the Exe Valley line passenger trains succumbed on 5th October 1963 (the official withdrawal date was 7th October) goods traffic, mainly bulk grain from Avonmouth, continued for a further three years.

A train to Exeter, hauled by 4575 Class 2-6-2T No.5524 running bunker-first, rolls into Up Exe Halt on 12th September 1959. When it opened in 1885 this station was known as 'Up Exe and Silverton', but the village of Silverton had its own station on the main Exeter to Taunton line, so the name was abbreviated in 1905. In October 1923 the station was converted to a halt without any staff.

Cadeleigh station, seen here in this portrait, is now the focal point of the Devon Railway Centre and is probably busier than at any stage in its career, although, sadly, today none of the customers are *bona fide* train travellers, merely tourists visiting a popular attraction. Prior to purchase for its new role the station and its environs were used as a highways depot for the local council. There was a passing loop here, controlled by the signal box on the left of the shot, while the goods shed, also on the left, is partially visible. Access to the shed was by means of a loop line that ran round the back of the northbound platform. When it opened the station was called 'Cadeleigh & Bickleigh' but this caused some confusion with Bickleigh station on the Plymouth to Launceston line and the name was shortened in 1906. Note the profusion of climbing rose bushes that really add to the station's charm. This picture was taken on 27th July 1963.

In this lovely pastoral scene, photographed in soft autumn sunshine, cows graze contentedly in the fields as an unidentified 0-6-0 pannier tank locomotive nears Bampton with a two-coach northbound train. This picture was taken on 13th October 1962. The coach formed immediately behind the locomotive is one of the 1951 series of auto-coaches, of which two carried names, *Thrush* and *Wren*. The vehicle depicted here is the former. While this line has always been known as the Exe Valley, this title is not entirely correct because for about a mile south of Bampton it follows the valley of the river Batherm which rises in the Brendon Hills, in Somerset.

Nestling in the valley of the river Batherm and surrounded by high hills on all sides, Bampton was as pretty a country station as one could wish to see. It was the terminating point of one or two trains from Exeter and in this picture an unidentified GWR-designed 0-6-0 pannier tank locomotive has just run round its train, probably the 4.25 from Exeter, and waits to shunt the coaches across to the southbound platform, from where it was booked to return to Exeter at 6.10pm. This photograph was taken in October 1962 and at that time the 6.10pm departure from Bampton was, by the modest standards of the Exe Valley line, quite a fast train; it omitted stops at some of the halts and reached its destination in fifty-six minutes. This shot appears to have been taken on a hazy, late summer day but the goods shed can clearly be seen and also the siding, on the extreme left, into a former limestone quarry which closed in about 1950. There was great sadness in the Exe Valley (and, presumably, in the Batherm Valley!) when the train service was withdrawn from 7th October 1963, the last services running on Saturday 5th October. The sadness of the local populace was probably heightened by the decision of the WR's operating authorities to replace the last trains, which would normally have been formed of former GWR 0-4-2Ts powering two coaches, with North British Type 2 diesel locomotives hauling six-coach rakes of open stock. At least the WR entered into the spirit of the occasion to some degree by running a few workings that would usually have run empty as passenger trains. The last train of all, hauled by Type 2 diesel No.D6343, left Bampton for Exeter at 11.00pm accompanied by a cacophony of exploding detonators, with the local band playing 'Auld Lang Syne.' After the train's departure everybody probably fell quiet and people were left to reflect that they would never again see a passenger train at that location.

G.W.R.

_____

Bampton
(DEVON)

Few branch lines featured in this album offered quite as much variety of scenery as the 34³/₄ miles-long line from Plymouth to Launceston. After passing the built-up suburbs of the city, the branch turned off the main Exeter line at Tavistock Junction and then threaded the thickly wooded Bickleigh Vale. Later, after leaving Tavistock, the line reached the wild and desolate western slopes of Dartmoor – the contrast could not be more marked. The broad gauge route between Plymouth and Tavistock was opened on 22nd June 1859 by the Tavistock & South Devon Railway. The success of this line prompted the people of Launceston to seek a rail connection with the outside world and the Launceston & South Devon Railway was opened on 1st July 1865. This line, also broad gauge, made an end-on connection with the former company at Tavistock. In this picture a Plymouth-bound train is seen standing at Shaugh Bridge platform, which was surrounded by dense woodland, in August 1962. This station was one of a number of new stopping places (most were described as a 'halt' or 'platform') on the Plymouth to Launceston line that were opened at various times, Shaugh Bridge opening on 21st August 1907, presumably for the benefit of hikers.

One of Laira shed's complement of 4575 Class 2-6-2Ts, No.5569, takes water at Lydford in time-honoured fashion while working a Launceston to Plymouth train in August 1962. This was the highest station on the line, 600ft above sea level, and it was superbly situated with Brent Tor to the south-west and Great Links Tor, 1,924ft, a towering backcloth on the eastern side of the line. The last day of passenger services on this outstanding route was Saturday 29th December 1962 (there was no Sunday service), a day that will be long-remembered because the Plymouth area suffered one of the worst blizzards in living memory that totally disrupted services on the Plymouth–Tavistock (South)–Launceston line. The 6.20pm Plymouth to Launceston started its journey more than an hour late and eventually arrived at Tavistock at 12.23am on Sunday 30th December, its journey having been delayed by a combination of frozen points, frozen brakes on the train and a small snowdrift at Grenofen tunnel. Twenty-five passengers on board spent the night in the train's first two coaches, with 4575 Class 2-6-2T locomotive No.5568 providing much needed heating, and they were taken on to their destinations by road the following day. Fifteen railway enthusiasts also spent the night in Tavistock and were eventually rescued from Tavistock (North) station by a special train from Plymouth, also the following day. Three passengers on the 7.10pm Tavistock (South) to Plymouth train spent the night in the signal box at Bickleigh after 0-6-0PT No.6400 had run out of water, and eventually reached Plymouth on the Sunday afternoon after a relief engine had been despatched from Laira. This was the last passenger train on the branch, a historic event that was probably not uppermost in the passengers' minds after such an ordeal.

PLYMOUTH TO LAUNCESTON

Apart from the two members of the train's crew posing for their photograph and three people peering out of carriage windows, Lydford station appears to have been totally deserted when this shot of a Plymouth-bound train was taken in August 1962. Lydford was served by both WR trains on the Plymouth–Tavistock (South)–Launceston line and SR services on the Plymouth–Tavistock (North)–Okehampton route, these lines running parallel between Tavistock and Lydford where each line had separate platforms, though it should be mentioned that the up SR Okehampton and down WR Plymouth platforms were adjoined. This duplication of routes and facilities was, almost needless to say, the result of pointless rivalry between pre-grouping companies and totally ignored the very sparse amount of traffic on offer in this remote and thinly populated area. The SR platforms are out of sight on the right of this picture. In the summer 1962 timetable a paltry five trains a day ran from Plymouth to Launceston and vice versa on Mondays to Fridays, with a further half a dozen 'short' workings to Tavistock (South). Services were more plentiful on the SR route but there were still long gaps between trains.

Coryton station, latterly known as Coryton Halt, was on the top section of the Launceston branch beyond Lydford, and was situated almost 'in the middle of nowhere', on the western edge of Dartmoor. It served a number of scattered hamlets and little else. Apart from the squat station building, the only other facilities there were a tiny goods yard complete with cattle pens, and a small ground frame. In this picture an unidentified GWR 2-6-2T is seen leaving with a two-coach train to Launceston, also in August 1962. The section between Lydford and Launceston was retained for goods traffic until 28th February 1966.

Isambard Kingdom Brunel – a truly great railway engineer. The bridge's centenary was commemorated by the unveiling of this plaque at Saltash station on 2nd May 1959.

The Royal Albert Bridge provides an immediate clue to the location of this photograph. It is, of course, Saltash station and this picture was taken on 2nd May 1959, a hundred years to the day after Isambard Kingdom Brunel's masterpiece was opened to traffic. At the time of this picture the railway, and a half-hourly chain ferry, provided the only means of crossing the river Tamar at this point and a shuttle service of auto-trains ran (in the summer 1961 timetable) to and from Plymouth between 5.30am and 11.15pm. In this illustration the 'road' ahead is clear for 6400 Class 0-6-0PT No.6420 from Laira shed and the station staff appear to be doing their utmost to get the train away. At first sight the train appears to be an ordinary passenger working, but in reality it is a Railway Correspondence & Travel Society rail tour of branches in the Plymouth area that had been organised in connection with the centenary. In addition to Saltash, the participants also visited the Turnchapel and Yealmpton branch lines. A train from London ran in connection with this tour and was hauled by 'Castle' class locomotives in each direction. By this date preparations were already being made on the Devon side for construction of the road bridge which eventually opened in October 1961, from which time the auto-train shuttle became a thing of the past. No.6420 was allocated to Laira shed for many years and one wonders how many times it must have crossed the famous bridge during its career.

SALTASH STATION AND THE ROYAL ALBERT BRIDGE

The Royal Albert Bridge strides majestically above the streets of Saltash. In 1845 Parliament rejected the plans of the Cornwall Railway (which eventually built the line between Plymouth and Truro) for a steam train ferry at Torpoint and the company turned to Brunel to survey alternative routes. He proposed a bridge which was an improved and enlarged version of his design for the crossing of the river Wye at Chepstow, and one of the most ambitious and complex civil engineering projects yet attempted. Each of the main spans is 455ft long and, due to the insistence of the Admiralty, they have 100ft clearance at high water. The spans, which were assembled on site, were floated into position and then gradually raised by jacks while the supporting piers were built. Originally, a double track bridge was planned but this was shelved in favour of a single track bridge resulting in a saving of £100,000. There are seven approach spans on the Devon side and ten on the Cornish bank of the river Tamar. The bridge was officially opened by Prince Albert on 2nd May 1859. Usually ladders and platforms, which are used to access the interior of the tubes, partially obscure the lettering on the end towers but BR removed them for the 1959 summer period to enable the wording to be clearly seen by onlookers. An especially attractive feature of the centenary celebrations was the fact that the main structure was illuminated at night. This view of the bridge, also taken on 2nd May 1959, gives some idea of its height in relation to the properties at ground level. During the Second World War a German invasion of the Devon/Cornwall peninsula was anticipated and the bridge was specially equipped with a flat surface between the rails to enable military vehicles to cross the river, there being few suitable road bridges across the Tamar. Road connections were made onto the track at each end of the bridge and locomotives were stationed on both sides to pull off any disabled army vehicles, using specially adapted chains.

The location is Liskeard main line station on the evening of Saturday 16th May 1959 and the principal subject is an auto-train of the type normally used on the Plymouth to Saltash shuttle service. It is likely that the train pictured is the 6.42pm Liskeard to Plymouth, which was the return working of the 5.35pm *ex*-Plymouth, due in Liskeard at 6.15pm. The shadows are encroaching and have almost totally obscured GWR 'Grange' Class 4-6-0 No.6845 *Paviland Grange* which is coming into the station on the down line with a westbound train, possibly the 6.10pm Plymouth to Penzance which was also due off Liskeard at 6.42pm. At this time No.6845 was based at Penzance, so it was at least heading in the right direction. The entrance from the up platform to the Looe branch platform is indicated by the white-painted fence, by the water tower.

Liskeard to Looe – a line of immense character. If there was ever a competition to find the most enchanting line in Cornwall, or even on the entire Western Region, the Looe branch would surely be a favourite to carry off the prize. It has a complex history, and its ancestry can be traced back to the Liskeard & Caradon Railway which opened from Mooorswater (in a valley west of Liskeard, adjacent to the Liskeard & Looe Union canal) to South Caradon in November 1844 and to Cheesewring quarries, on the edge of Bodmin Moor, in March 1846. Wagons loaded with minerals descended by gravity and were worked back up the hill by horses. In December 1860 an extension of the line was opened by the canal company along the bank of the canal to Looe, and from 1862 it was worked by the Caradon Railway. The line's principal purpose was the conveyance of mineral traffic but passengers were carried in open wagons until normal passenger-carrying operations commenced on 11th September 1879. The line operated in splendid isolation from the main line until the GWR constructed a sharply graded loop line from Coombe Junction to a separate branch terminus at right angles to the main Liskeard station in May 1901. The Looe branch platform is seen in this picture which was taken on 2nd May 1959.

The line from Coombe Junction to Liskeard, as previously mentioned, ascends very steeply from the junction, almost like a spiral. This picture, which shows former GWR 2-6-2T No.5523 approaching Liskeard branch platform with a train from Looe on 17th May 1959, gives a hint of the tortuous and very hilly nature of this part of the branch. Note the spare carriages in the siding on the right which could be immediately pressed into service when the need arose.

The view from a window of a train climbing towards Liskeard on 17th May 1959, with No.5523 no doubt working very hard at the front of the train.

Looking more like an aerial view of a model railway layout than the real thing, here is a stunning portrait of the locomotive and carriage & wagon workshops at Moorswater taken from an open window of a main line train crossing Moorswater viaduct on 2nd May 1959. The tracks in the foreground lead to Coombe Junction, where passenger trains between Liskeard and Looe had to reverse, while the course of the old line to Caradon appears to be indicated by the line of trees on the left of the picture. The road on the extreme right of the shot leads to Liskeard town centre. The workshops here were constructed in about 1861 to serve the Liskeard & Looe and Liskeard & Caradon railways, which made an end-on connection at this point, and the shed was retained by the GWR when it took over the working of both lines in 1909. The Caradon line lasted until 1916 while the sidings from the station to the quay at Looe, where boats were once loaded with tin ore and granite, have also gone.

A train bound for Looe makes its way sedately southwards between Sandplace and Looe on 17th May 1959; 4575 Class 2-6-2T No.5523 provides the motive power. The branch runs parallel to the Looe river almost all of the way from Coombe Junction and provides – at least for travellers with time on their hands – one of the most relaxing and enjoyable journeys one could wish for.

Opposite: A picture looking towards Coombe Junction Halt, which is out of sight behind the train, with the elegant Moorswater viaduct dominating the scene in the background. The train is signalled for the Liskeard line. One wonders whether any photographer was lucky enough to obtain a shot showing a main line train crossing the viaduct as a Looe branch working pulled away from Coombe Junction Halt. This picture appears to have been taken from Coombe Junction signal box at which there was a sign indicating a speed limit of 15mph for trains passing the box. The signal box at Coombe Junction was located in a peaceful and tranquil setting, the signalman being only occasionally disturbed by branch trains and the odd light engine movement to Moorswater shed – quite a contrast to Liskeard main line box on a summer Saturday. The line to Moorswater shed continues straight ahead and disappears under the bridge and main line viaduct.

Looe station occupies a cramped site sandwiched between the hilly town and the river. This view was taken looking northwards, with the river estuary on the left, and depicts 2-6-2T No.5523 apparently pulling forward onto the loop in the foreground prior to running round its train. At that time the railway sidings still occupied the strip of land between the road and river bank all of the way down to the road bridge connecting East and West Looe, the sidings being a reminder of more prosperous times when minerals were trans-shipped at the quay. This picture was taken on 17th May 1959 and scenes such as this, with steam traction, continued until the end of the summer 1961 timetable when the branch was dieselised. The railway's impact on the town of Looe may have been vastly different if a proposal by the GWR had ever come to fruition. In 1935 they planned a completely new line from St Germans to East Looe, the terminus being conveniently sited near a new hotel that was being proposed by the company, and a frequent commuter service to and from Plymouth was apparently envisaged using diesel railcars. The plans were soon abandoned due to the cost of the heavy earthworks required.

2nd - PRIVILEGE RETURN	PRIVILEGE - 2nd RETURN
Looe to	Liskeard to
LISKEARD	**LOOE**
(W) Fare 1/3 (0·06)	Fare 1/3 (0·06) (W)
For conditions see over	For conditions see over

7920 P P M 7920

The Lostwithiel & Fowey Railway opened a broad-gauge goods-only line between Lostwithiel and Carne Point, just outside Fowey, on 1st June 1869, the principal traffic being clay. In June 1874 a rival line from St Blazey to Fowey opened for business and the two routes were locked in fierce competition, with the result that that the Lostwithiel & Fowey Railway was forced to close on 1st January 1880. The line was eventually reopened throughout to Fowey, as a standard gauge route, on 16th September 1895 and for the first time it conveyed both passenger and goods traffic. Ordinary passengers were carried between St Blazey and Fowey until 1929, from which time a workmen's service only was provided until it, too, was discontinued at the end of 1934, but the line remained open for goods until it was converted into a road in 1968. In this illustration Lostwithiel station is seen on 16th May 1959 with former GWR 0-4-2T No.1419 simmering in the far platform before leaving with the Fowey branch train. The station was kept in a very tidy condition and there was even a palm tree on the platform which gave the place a continental air.

A scene at Fowey station on the same day the previous shots were taken, with No.1419 getting down to some energetic shunting work. It is likely that No.1419 was merely dropping back into the bay platform to allow an empty clay train from the jetties, which were located beyond the station, to pass. While the ordinary passenger service from Fowey to St Blazey was taken off as long ago as 1929, as previously mentioned, the branch trains to and from Lostwithiel lasted until they succumbed on 4th January 1965.

A scene on 'Southern' metals at Wadebridge, showing former GWR 2-6-2T No.5519 awaiting departure with a train to Bodmin Road (later Bodmin Parkway) on 2nd May 1959. Most Western Region services ran between Wadebridge and Bodmin Road, while the Southern Region trains to and from Bodmin North served intermediate stations, so the pattern of services between these two medium-sized towns was quite complicated, at least to the uninitiated! There was a small locomotive shed at Wadebridge which was a place of pilgrimage for railway enthusiasts because it was home to the three surviving Beattie well tank 2-4-0 locomotives that were employed on the Wenfordbridge mineral line. In addition, at the time of this photograph some veteran LSWR T9 Class 4-4-0s were still active on trains over the North Cornwall line to Okehampton, so Wadebridge was a really absorbing spot for the steam enthusiast. Sadly, there is no railway presence at all in the town today, all passenger trains being withdrawn from 30th January 1967 whilst goods traffic lingered until the late-1970s.

The history of the Bodmin Road to Bodmin General line can be traced back to 27th May 1887 when it started operation largely as a feeder to the main line. Just over a year later, on 3rd September 1888, an extension was opened to (what later became) Boscarne Junction, on the Bodmin & Wadebridge Railway, which began life puffing along the wooded valley of the river Camel way back in 1834. This line transported mainly sea-sand, china clay and granite and was the first railway in Cornwall. Few stations depicted in this album have quite the irresistible appeal of Bodmin General, with its compact layout, stone-built station building and, at the time of this photograph, an expertly maintained rockery. The unwary may at first sight think this was a branch line terminus but, in reality, it was merely an intermediate station on the route between Bodmin Road and Wadebridge, where locomotives were obliged to run round their trains. The station is now the headquarters of the Bodmin & Wenford Railway and surely ranks as one of the most attractive and distinctive preserved stations in Great Britain. Sadly, before the preservationists arrived on the scene BR unceremoniously demolished the engine shed, formerly a sub-shed of St Blazey, goods shed and signal box, all of which had greatly added to the station's character and undoubted charm. This picture was taken on 2nd May 1959.

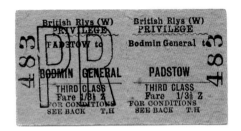

After several false starts the Helston Railway Company obtained its Act on 9th July 1880 for the construction of an 8¾ miles-long line from Gwinear Road, on the main line west of Camborne, to the town of Helston, the focal point of the Lizard peninsula. The GWR was involved from the outset and covenanted to provide staff, motive power and rolling stock, and also agreed to maintain the permanent way for a trial period. The line was opened to traffic on 9th May 1887 and it is recorded that the first train, suitably decorated with flags and foliage, left Helston at 9.40am amid much celebration. The line was vested in the GWR on 1st July 1898. Besides having Great Britain's most southerly station, the branch also had a particular claim to fame because the very first railway-worked omnibus service operated from Helston station to the Lizard. It had been the intention eventually to extend the line to the Lizard, and Helston station was built as a through station with this in mind, but the bus service, which began on 17th August 1903, was extremely successful and put paid to the railway extension for which parliamentary authority had already been obtained. The line had an uneventful existence but in 1961 rumours started to circulate regarding its future, and, despite a vigorous anti-closure campaign, the government of the day sanctioned closure from 5th November 1962. The last passenger trains actually ran on 3rd November, the last train being made up of six coaches hauled by North British Type 2 diesel locomotive No.D6312 and, sadly, the branch became the first in Cornwall to lose its passenger service since before the Second World War – a very dubious distinction. Goods traffic survived somewhat longer, the last official train running on 3rd October 1964 with Type 2 No.D6324 in charge; the same locomotive collected all remaining stock on 9th October. This shot was taken at Gwinear Road station on 16th May 1959 with No.4564 simmering on a Helston train.

Helston station is seen in this photograph, looking towards Gwinear Road, on the same day as the previous illustration; the locomotive is, once again, *ex*-GWR 4500 Class 2-6-2T No.4564. The station here was built, as previously stated, as a through station and the tracks behind the photographer continued for about 200 yards along an embankment which was obviously built with the extension to the Lizard very much in mind. There used to be a carriage shed on the embankment but this was dismantled in about 1958. The station had only a single platform, as seen here, and boasted a privately-owned refreshment room which was advertised with a huge sign on the side wall of the station, but the main purpose of the building does not appear to be indicated. First time visitors to the establishment may have been surprised to find that the refreshment room had a station 'attached'! Note the flower tubs on the platform and telephone booth, all of which add a further splash of colour to the scene.

Platform trolleys and barrows litter the Gwinear Road end of Helston station, also on 16th May 1959. The signal box is prominent in the centre of this shot as former GWR 2-6-2T 4500 Class No.4564 comes off the shed, presumably to work a train back to Gwinear Road. At the time of this photograph No.4564 was based at St Blazey shed, about forty miles away by rail from Helston, so it probably spent protracted periods away from its home depot. Helston was a sub-shed of Penzance and was doubtless used to stable the branch engine overnight.

The late Chris Gammell, the well-known railway photographer, author and publisher, was a connoisseur of British branch lines and once said that the 4¼ miles-long branch from St Erth to St Ives was unquestionably his favourite line – and no wonder! Most of the line runs on a narrow ledge cut into the cliffs and trains have to negotiate tortuous curves as the track twists and turns around the headlands. In addition to the extreme curvature, enginemen also had to contend with some fierce gradients, some as steep as 1 in 60. While working a steam train along the line may have been a challenge for the crew on the footplate, particularly if the rails were slippery due to sea spray or mist, the experience of a trip on the branch for passengers was entirely different, especially on a clear day when some of the views across the bay were absolutely magical and breathtaking. This wonderfully scenic line dates back to 1st June 1877, when it opened for business. It was the last branch built to the broad gauge. This vintage road sign was photographed near St Erth station on 16th May 1959.

A train bound for the main-line junction at St Erth accelerates away from Carbis Bay station on 16th May 1959, with 4500 Class 2-6-2T No.4563 providing the motive power. Note that the station building at this location was built above the platform, presumably to avoid a lot of unnecessary work excavating the deep cutting at this spot. Facilities on the platform consisted merely of a waiting shelter which is visible above the second coach of the train.

Blue horizons. The scene that every holiday-maker dreams of – a clear blue sky with uninterrupted sunshine, sea as blue as blue can be and inviting soft golden sands. Certainly, when this shot was taken overlooking St Ives station all of those criteria were fulfilled, but the author is unaware of the air temperature on 16th May 1959, when the picture was taken. Certainly there is plenty of room on the beach, which suggests it may not have been as warm as it appears. The course of the railway is marked by the signals in the foreground above the bushes. At the station a 4500 Class locomotive appears to be running round its two-coach train.

A portrait of St Ives station on 16th May 1959 with No.4563 waiting to leave for St Erth. During the peak summer months the branch was worked by three locomotives in order to avoid losing time when running round at each end of the line. Steam traction lasted until the end of the 1961 summer timetable and it is reported that the last engine to be serviced at the small engine shed at St Ives was No.4564 which is depicted elsewhere in this album. In addition to the long, curving main platform at St Ives there was also a bay platform which is out of camera range.

A passenger's eye-view of St Ives station on 16th May 1959. A young man appears to be loitering at the Wymans' newspaper kiosk while a lady searches for her purse. On the left 4500 Class engine No.4563 simmers prior to departure for St Erth. At that time the station provided a wealth of facilities: there was a ticket office, waiting rooms, public toilets and even a telephone booth from where 'lost' holiday-makers could summon a taxi to take them to their hotel. Note the camping coach in the middle of the picture. BR was clearly doing its utmost to cater for all classes of visitor by offering a wide range of accommodation from the rather rudimentary facilities in the camping coach seen here or rooms at the plush and sophisticated Tregenna Castle. The latter, purchased by the GWR in 1878, was converted into a hotel and no doubt became the preserve of those who appreciated a little luxury. But, perhaps holidays were more fun in a camping coach and much less of a strain on one's wallet!

BRITISH RLYS. (Western Region) (4237)
TO
ST. IVES

3rd-SINGLE   SINGLE-3rd
St. Ives to
St Ives   St Ives
St. Erth   St. Erth
ST.ERTH
(W)   9d H   FARE   9d H   (W)
For Conditions see over   For Conditions see over
8734   8734

The Malmesbury branch has a particularly interesting history and is probably unique in that its junction was changed from one main line to another of equal importance. The earliest scheme to refer to Malmesbury was mooted in 1863 by the Wiltshire & Gloucestershire Railway which planned a line linking Christian Malford, near Chippenham, with Nailsworth but this idea soon faltered. In contrast the plans of the Malmesbury Railway, which obtained an Act on 25th July 1872 to construct a 6½ miles-long line from Dauntsey, between Swindon and Chippenham, to Malmesbury soon came to fruition. The line was formally opened 'amid much rejoicings' on 17th December 1877; the building work is reported to have cost around £60,000 and the line was worked by the GWR from the start. The branch was taken over by the GWR on 1st July 1880. The Badminton route, a shorter line from Wootton Bassett to the Severn tunnel than the route via Bristol, was opened on 1st July 1903. Nearly thirty years later it was decided to lay a connection from near Little Somerford station, on the 'new' line, and this was completed by 6th February 1933, but a legal technicality delayed opening until 17th July 1933, from which date the line to Dauntsey was closed. The length of the branch was reduced to 3¾ miles. The branch led an uneventful life and latterly there were five weekday trains in each direction. The passenger service was an early casualty, being withdrawn from 10th September 1951, but goods traffic continued for a further eleven years until this ceased to operate from 12th November 1962. Malmesbury had stone-built station buildings, a small engine shed with a water tower and the usual goods facilities. The entire layout had Malmesbury Abbey, on a higher level, as a striking backdrop which can be seen in this shot of 5800 Class 0-4-2T No.5815, posing amid the ruins of Malmesbury station on a misty 29th October 1960. By that time No.5815 was the last surviving member of its class and was regularly employed on the branch goods six days a week. It did not, however, survive to work the last train because the branch goods was powered by a small diesel shunter for the last couple of years.

A damp day at Kingham – 27th August 1960. The fireman of GWR-designed 'Hall' Class 4-6-0 No.7928 *Wolf Hall* has obviously just put a shovelful of coal onto the engine's fire in preparation for the next stage of the journey towards Oxford. The train has the 'road' and has just started to pull out of the station, but the guard seems to be a trifle slow returning to his van and he has not yet closed the door. Note the colourful flower displays, the notice requesting passengers to cross the line by the bridge and the giant telegraph poles.

Kingham station was once an important junction and passengers were left in no doubt about its status by the running-in boards, which originally proclaimed 'Kingham change for Chipping Norton, Bourton-on-the-Water, Banbury and Cheltenham Lines'. When this picture was taken on 6th October 1962, the service beyond Chipping Norton to Banbury had long been abandoned and 'Banbury' had been painted over as a destination on the board. Sadly, more paint would have been needed before the end of the year because services on the Cheltenham and Chipping Norton lines were about to be axed. The line through Kingham was opened by the Oxford, Worcester & Wolverhampton Railway (OW&WR) on 4th June 1853 and the station began life on 10th August 1855, being located at the point where the branch from Chipping Norton joined the OW&WR. Predictably, the station was called Chipping Norton Junction and this

name was used until it was changed to Kingham on 1st May 1909. In 1862 a branch to Bourton-on-the-Water was opened, this being extended to Cheltenham in 1881. The station consisted of four platforms but it should be noted that there was no facing connection off the main line to the Chipping Norton branch. Through trains between Banbury and Chippenham had to reverse in the station and this procedure continued until a flyover was opened north of the station in 1906. The station's importance can be judged from the fact that there was a small engine shed and turntable and, in the mid-1950s, fifty-two trains were scheduled to arrive or depart each weekday. Like many country stations Kingham had periods of feverish activity when branch services arrived to meet main line trains and then went into a slumber for a while until the next busy period. This photograph which, as previously mentioned, dates from October 1962 shows the Chipping Norton platforms with a train apparently awaiting departure.

Goodbye to trains to Chipping Norton. This picture of 5101 Class 2-6-2T No.4101 waiting to leave Kingham with a service to Chipping Norton was also taken on 6th October 1962 during the final three months of operation, the branch closing to passengers from 3rd December 1962. By this time the train service on the branch had been reduced to just two trains per day and, perhaps, could be fairly described as a token service. The line once ran through to Banbury (Kings Sutton) but this section was closed to passenger traffic as long ago as 4th June 1951 while goods trains continued to operate on part of the route beyond Chipping Norton until around 1963. Note the main-line coaching stock.

The Fairford branch line was built in two stages by entirely separate railway companies. The people of the prosperous blanket manufacturing town of Witney had long desired a connection with the booming railway network but the GWR were unhelpful and thwarted various schemes. In December 1858 a meeting was held in the town and the independent Witney Railway Co. was formed. On 1st August 1859 the Royal assent was granted to a bill to build a single-track line from the Oxford, Worcester & Wolverhampton Railway at Yarnton to Witney. The line was opened amid much rejoicing on 13th November 1861. This picture shows the compact little station at Witney, looking towards Fairford, in February 1962.

The East Gloucestershire Railway had originally planned to link Witney with Cheltenham via Andoversford but this ambitious plan was shelved in favour of a purely local line from Witney to Fairford. The line was opened on 14th January 1873 and the entire 22 miles-long Fairford branch was operated by the GWR until that company took over both local concerns in 1890. The line led an unremarkable life serving the local community and witnessed an increase in traffic during the Second World War due to the number of military personnel travelling to and from various bases along the route. After the war, however, the huge increase in private motoring steadily eroded traffic and the line was closed to passengers from 18th June 1962, the last trains running on 16th June. The section beyond Witney was closed completely, but goods traffic continued on the Oxford to Witney stretch until it, too, succumbed in November 1970. The branch was once described as 'terminating in a meadow' and certainly there is little habitation visible in this photograph of Fairford station which was also taken in February 1962. There was, however, a small engine shed west of the station. Fairford was built as a through station, the layout indicating that the East Gloucestershire Railway still harboured ambitious plans to reach Cheltenham, a dream that was never fulfilled.

An afternoon train to Kemble, with former GWR 8750 Class 0-6-0PT No.8783 in charge, leaves Cirencester Town station on 24th January 1959, during the penultimate week of steam operation. The last ordinary steam passenger train was the 11.30pm Cirencester Town to Kemble and 12.05am return on 1st February with No.9672 providing the motive power. The replacement railbus, No.W79975, apparently failed on its first day in service on the branch, but the problem was quickly rectified.

The last act on the Cirencester branch. Almost 123 years of railway service came to an end on the night of 5th/6th April 1964 when the final trains ran on the Cirencester branch. The last services were the 11.30pm from Cirencester Town station and 12.05am return from Kemble, which connected with the 9.25pm (previous day) train from Paddington. Both services were formed of diesel railbus No.W79977. Earlier in the day a steam-hauled special, formed of GWR-designed 0-4-2T No.1472 and a Chalford rail-motor set, covered both the Tetbury and Cirencester branches and became the last steam-hauled train to leave Town station. Here, No.1472 poses in the spring sunshine against the attractive backdrop of Cirencester Town station's lovely ornate Gothic-style station building.

The last days of steam on the Kemble to Tetbury branch. GWR 0-4-2T No.1417 waits in the bay at Kemble prior to leaving with a train to Tetbury on 24th January 1959, while a brand new railbus rests in a siding between test runs. The last steam train to leave Tetbury was the 6.05pm to Kemble on 31st January with 5800 Class 0-4-2T No.5804 in charge. It is reported that following local publicity a large crowd turned out to travel on the train, known locally as the 'Tetbury Donkey', which left to the accompaniment of cheers and waving, not to mention the deafening sound of about a dozen detonators being exploded. There were fun and games on the return 6.45pm *ex*-Kemble which made an unofficial stop at Trouble House Halt, a new station that had been built to boost the new diesel service and was not supposed to open officially until two days later! People on the train retired to the local hostelry while No.5804 simmered at the station. The structure partially visible above the locomotive is Kemble station's famous water tank that has been a local landmark since 1903. This structure actually consists of two tanks, the top of the main one being 29ft. above rail level while the smaller tank was 60ft aloft. The first line through Kemble ran to Cirencester and was opened by the Cheltenham & Great Western Union Railway on 31st May 1841.

The Tetbury branch operated from 2nd December 1889 to 5th April 1964. Many branch lines have as their founding fathers a group of local worthies who wished to see their town connected to the railway system, but in this case the branch was not proposed by local entrepreneurs but by the GWR. The railbus depicted in this shot taken at Tetbury station on 21st March 1964, is thought to be No.W79977 which was damaged at Swindon at some time and emerged from repair in an odd shade of green, with a yellow warning panel and a white domed roof. The last services on the branch were worked by No.W79978, however, on 4th April and it is recorded that a coffin addressed to Doctor Beeching was loaded aboard the final train at Trouble House Halt and transferred to a London-bound express at Kemble. The very last train to leave Tetbury, which had already lost its goods service, was a special the following day with former GWR 0-4-2T No.1472 in charge of a Chalford rail-motor set.

There can be no doubt whatsoever regarding the location, but perhaps it should be pointed out that by the date of this photograph, 12th September 1964, the Great Western Railway had long since faded into history. The train disappearing into the distance is a Gloucester Central to Chalford auto-train. This service, which served twelve stations and halts in sixteen miles, had the character of a branch line operation but ran along the tracks of the Gloucester to Swindon main line.

The GWR-designed 1400 Class 0-4-2Ts were, as previously stated, normally rostered to work the Chalford motor-trains and by the autumn of 1964 the bulk of the class were based at Gloucester shed for these duties. In this illustration an unidentified example is seen near Stroud with one of these trains. Some of the halts on this picturesque route boasted GWR 'pagoda' waiting shelters but others had nothing more than basic 'tin shacks' which at least provided some protection from the elements. The withdrawal of the Chalford trains, and those on the Berkeley Road to Sharpness line, marked the end of the former GWR rail-motor services. It was not, however, the final demise of these auto-trains because the Yeovil Junction to Yeovil Town service, which the WR inherited in the 1963 boundary changes, was still regularly operated by rail-motor sets. The *very last* services of this type are thought to have been those on the Seaton branch, in Devon, where auto-trains operated for a brief period in February 1965 due to a shortage of diesel units. Locomotives in use on the Chalford service on the last day of services, 31st October 1964, included 1400 Class 0-4-2Ts Nos.1458 and 1472 plus 6400 Class 0-6-0PT No.6412.

The Chalford auto-trains usually employed 1400 Class 0-4-2Ts on two-coach trains and these locomotives remained staple power until the service was withdrawn on 2nd November 1964. Only seven 1400 Class engines remained in traffic in October 1964, five of which were allocated to Gloucester (Horton Road) shed, so the Chalford trains were one of their last strongholds; the remaining two locomotives were based at Yeovil. Not all Gloucester to Chalford workings were covered by 1400 Class locomotives, however, and in this view 8750 Class 0-6-0 pannier tank engine No.3681 waits in Stroud station with one of these trains, on 12th September 1964, before proceeding up the scenic Golden Valley. The steam rail-motor service was introduced by the GWR on this section in 1903 and later became an everyday feature of operations throughout their system.

The Gloucester to Swindon line is very heavily graded and climbs all of the way from Stroud to a summit inside Sapperton tunnel: some of the gradients are as steep as 1 in 60. There was a pressing need to economise on building costs and the course of the line was apparently chosen against the advice of Brunel, who favoured a different route with easier gradients. Consequently, generations of railwaymen have been faced with the formidable task of working over the route and doubtless wished Brunel's opinion had prevailed, which would have made life easier. Passengers with time on their hands probably approved of the route, however, because the slow progress made by eastbound trains as they toiled up the Golden Valley towards Sapperton tunnel merely gave them more time to admire the beautiful scenery. The grades meant that eastbound heavy goods trains had to be assisted and banking engines were normally based at Brimscombe where they were stabled in a small depot, this being a sub-shed of Gloucester (Horton Road). In this September 1964 view an unidentified GWR 'Mogul' is visible on Brimscombe shed between banking duties while a rather grimy 'Castle' Class 4-6-0, No.7022 *Hereford Castle,* descends the steep bank down from Sapperton tunnel with a goods train. Note the signal beyond the 'Mogul' which apparently controlled movements from the engine shed onto the main line.

The 14³/₄ miles-long Wye Valley line linked Chepstow with Monmouth and was opened by the Wye Valley Railway Co. (WVR) on 1st November 1876. The company had obtained an Act of Parliament ten years earlier but progress was halted by a financial crisis at that time. The southern part of the line required heavy engineering works, the 1188 yards-long tunnel at Tidenham being especially noteworthy. The line was operated from the start by the GWR but it was not financially successful, the WVR being declared bankrupt more than once during its relatively brief existence, and the GWR took over the entire operation in 1905. The largest intermediate station on the line was Tintern which had three platforms, this reflecting the desire of the promoters to develop tourist traffic to the nearby Tintern abbey. There was a short branch here across the river Wye to a wire works which was operational between 1876 and 1935. The scenic delights of the Wye valley can be appreciated from this shot of Tintern station that was taken on 16th August 1958 with a local goods train in the northbound platform. The passenger service lasted until 5th January 1959 and goods trains continued to serve Tintern quarry until 1981. The station here is in a particularly attractive setting and was later developed as a tourist attraction in its own right, with an exhibition about the line, small café, and craft shop in the old signal box. Two carriages are located here and, apparently, there is even a working set of semaphore signals!

More stunning scenery in the Wye valley. In this August 1958 picture Brockweir Halt can be seen on the left of the shot. In the 1920s/30s the GWR opened several halts on the line, presumably in a bid to attract more traffic at a time when road competition was developing. The halt seen here was obviously cheaply built, the platform being of the standard 'wood and ash' type with a rudimentary corrugated waiting shelter. Brockweir Halt dated from 1929 and one wonders how many passengers it saw during its brief thirty-year career.

A magnificent panoramic photograph of Monmouth (Troy) and the surrounding landscape taken from above the tunnel just west of the station on 16th August 1958. The Wye Valley line diverges to the right adjacent to the signal box, which is just visible beyond the water tank, and crosses a valley on a superb viaduct originally built for the Coleford, Monmouth, Usk and Pontypool Railway in 1857 by Joseph Firbank, a well-known civil engineer. The line going off to the left, which crosses the river Wye on a girder bridge, leads to Ross-on-Wye via Symonds Yat, as pretty a railway journey as one could wish for. Monmouth (Troy) was a typical GWR country station with stone buildings, corrugated iron sheds, gas lamps and lower quadrant signals. In 1885 an ambitious plan was put forward by the Midland Railway for a line deep into GWR territory which would have passed through Monmouth, but the scheme failed to get off the ground. A noteworthy event occurred in 1910 when the funeral train of C.S. Rolls, of the world famous Rolls Royce engineering company, used Monmouth (Troy) station. The station's decline really started in 1955 when the line to Pontypool Road was closed and four years later, from 5th January 1959, passenger services were withdrawn from both the Wye Valley and Ross-on-Wye routes, the last train over both lines being a Stephenson Locomotive Society special hauled by a brace of GWR pannier tank engines. Goods traffic lingered until 1964, after which time Monmouth was sadly erased from the railway map.

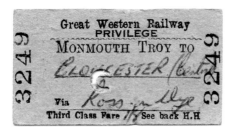

The 22½ miles-long broad gauge line from Gloucester (Grange Court Junction) to Hereford via Ross-on-Wye was opened by the Hereford, Ross and Gloucester Railway on 1st June 1855. There were seven intermediate stations on the line at first, while three halts were later added in GWR days. The company was amalgamated with the GWR in 1862 and seven years later the line was converted to standard gauge, becoming one of the first to be altered. Initially, there were around half-a-dozen weekday passenger trains a day in each direction. The 'Illustrated London News', dated 14th July 1855, hailed the opening of the line, stating that it provided 'cheap and easy access' for the masses to one of the finest rivers in Europe, which had previously been 'a treat only within the reach of the wealthy'. Unfortunately, in later years their enthusiasm does not appear to have been shared by the travelling public and in the mid-1950s the line had a meagre service of only eight weekday trains each way, which was presumably considered adequate for the amount of traffic on offer. In later years the route came under the wretched Beeching axe, services being withdrawn from 2nd November 1964 with the final trains running on 31st October. In this picture, taken on 19th September 1964, a Hereford-bound train has just emerged from Ballingham tunnel, between Ballingham and Holme Lacy stations. Towards the end of steam most WR motive power was in a parlous state and the unidentified 'Manor' Class 4-6-0 seen here is in absolutely appalling external condition.

North of Ross-on-Wye the Gloucester to Hereford line crossed and re-crossed the river Wye four times before it reached its destination. The river meandered southwards through lush and fertile countryside which is clearly apparent here as the train depicted in the previous shot steams towards its next station stop at Holme Lacy. Most trains on this rural line stopped at all stations and took around 1¼ hours to cover the thirty miles between Gloucester and Hereford, so it was not a trip for travellers in a hurry but much more suitable for those aficionados who merely wished to admire the delightful pastoral scenery through which the line passed.

The Bewdley to Woofferton line was a real gem and even the names of places served by the route – Neen Sollars, Cleobury Mortimer and Tenbury Wells – give a hint of its undoubted attractions. In addition, the line penetrated deep into the Wyre Forest, parts of which were inaccessible by car. The Tenbury Wells to Woofferton stretch was the first to be built, the Tenbury Railway, a short-lived local company, obtaining an Act on 21st July 1859 and the line was opened by the Shrewsbury & Hereford Railway on 1st August 1861. This line is probably unique in that it lasted exactly a century, closing completely on 31st July 1961. The last trains ran on 29th July, the final services being the specially strengthened 6.23pm from Kidderminster to Woofferton and 7.38pm return to Bewdley, which were powered by 6100 Class 2-6-2T No.6144 carrying a commemorative wreath and placard. The line between Bewdley and Tenbury Wells was promoted by the Tenbury & Bewdley Railway and opened on 13th August 1864; it was worked

from the beginning by the GWR which absorbed the local company in 1869. When the service was withdrawn from the section west of Tenbury Wells, the number of trains between Tenbury Wells and Bewdley was drastically reduced to one per day on Mondays to Fridays only. BR agreed to maintain this service, mainly for the benefit of schoolchildren, on condition that if it was poorly patronised it would be withdrawn after twelve months. These trains were the 7.55am from Tenbury Wells to Kidderminster and 4.10pm return. The services last ran on Tuesday 31st July 1962, this being a most unusual case of a branch service being withdrawn in the middle of the week, and it is recorded that the last train was hauled by 8750 Class 0-6-0PT No.3619 hauling two coaches. In this picture a small crowd of passengers awaits the arrival of GWR railcar No.W22W at Wyre Forest station on 1st April 1961. Note the gentleman carrying the stakes; surely he was not intending to take them on the train!

The waiting shelter, conical-shaped water tank and lower quadrant signals, plus a GWR railcar really complete this picture of a GWR station that had clearly remained untouched for years. There was no mistaking the origins of Cleobury Mortimer station, seen here in this portrait taken on the same date as the previous shot. Note the ancient grounded horsebox on the down platform. This station was well known as the starting point of the Cleobury Mortimer and Ditton Priors Light Railway, whose platform was adjacent to the premises seen here. It opened to goods traffic on 19th July 1908 while passenger operations commenced on 20th November of that year. Passenger trains were withdrawn as long ago as 26th September 1938 and the Admiralty, which had an armaments depot at Ditton Priors, took over operation in 1957. The line was finally closed in 1965.

The little station of Neen Sollars, which served a nearby hamlet of the same name, was hidden away in the south Shropshire countryside and was doubtless one of the smallest and most remote rural stations in Great Britain. In the mid-1950s, when most of the population still relied upon public transport to get around, Neen Sollars had a meagre weekday train service of six workings each way and, presumably, most trains were formed of GWR railcars, these being advertised in the timetable as offering 'limited accommodation' – hardly an inducement to travel! Despite a large amount of cloud in the sky, the photographer managed to capture GWR railcar No.W32W in glorious sunshine, on 30th July 1960. Note the recently relaid track: it was often alleged that BR deliberately relaid lines they wished to close because the outlay could distort the running costs of a branch line and tip the balance in favour of closure.

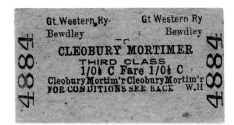

After the storm. Photographed in absolutely brilliant lighting conditions, Tenbury Wells station is pictured here on 30th July 1960 with menacing dark storm clouds as a backdrop. BR had hoped to cease passenger operations over the entire Bewdley to Woofferton line in July 1961 but, apparently in response to local protests, a token service of one train each way on Mondays to Fridays was retained over the Bewdley to Tenbury Wells section. When this ended a year later the goods service continued until 6th January 1964, when it was cut back to Cleobury Mortimer. The solidly-built station here was later demolished and the site cleared to make way for an industrial estate.

(4237)
BRITISH RYS. (Western Region)
TO
Tenbury Wells

BEWDLEY TO WOOFFERTON

This view, taken from the northbound platform at Bewdley station, will be familiar to many readers who have visited the Severn Valley Railway, one of the longest and most successful preserved lines in Great Britain. When this picture was taken, however, on 30th July 1960, Bewdley station was still very much part of the BR system and served by regular branch services, northwards to Shrewsbury via Bridgnorth and southwards to Kidderminster plus Worcester. Here, a GWR railcar waits as a pannier tank engine approaches at the head of a passenger working. The original Severn Valley Railway Co. (SVR) obtained its Act in 1853 authorising construction of the line between Hartlebury and Shrewsbury, a distance of 40¾ miles. The standard gauge line was single throughout and numerous civil engineering works were required, including the magnificent bridge across the river Severn at Arley and the 594 yards-long tunnel to take the track under the town at Bridgnorth. Regular services began between Hartlebury and Shrewsbury on 1st February 1862 and just over ten years later, on 18th July 1872, the SVR was absorbed into the GWR, which opened the link from Bewdley to Kidderminster in 1878. Despite considerable coal traffic from Highley, and agricultural

produce, the line eventually proved to be uneconomic and, after years of declining receipts, the section from Bewdley to Shrewsbury was closed to passengers from 9th September 1963.

A further shot taken at Bewdley station, this time on 1st April 1961, with a GWR railcar in the principal southbound platform. After the main part of the Severn Valley line was closed to passenger traffic, the section from Alveley colliery (Highley) to Buildwas remained open for coal trains for a short time but this was closed on 30th November 1963, while the mine's last rail link, southwards to Bewdley, was shut from 3rd February 1969. A sparse service of passenger trains continued to run southwards from Bewdley until 3rd January 1970 when services ceased on the lines to both Kidderminster and Hartlebury.

Coalport station is seen in this illustration, with a small part of the river Severn just visible in the background. This picture was also taken on 1st April 1961. In the summer 1961 public timetable Coalport station was served by a derisory five trains every weekday and some of those were formed of GWR railcars which had very limited seating capacity; there were no trains on Sundays. The rails almost seem to have a thin layer of rust – surely not? In addition to a station on the Severn Valley line, Coalport was served by a London & North Western Railway branch from Wellington (Hadley Junction) to Coalport East station, which was located just across the river from the station seen here.

Some services along the Severn Valley line were, as previously mentioned, formed of GWR railcars and in this picture one of these splendid contraptions is depicted near Coalport forming a northbound train. The first successful GWR railcar was introduced in 1933 and in the spring of 1961, towards the end of railcar operation, all surviving cars were transferred to Worcester and the Severn Valley line became one of their last haunts, the remaining examples being withdrawn in October 1962. The line was certainly the last haunt of railcar No.W10W which caught fire at Bridgnorth on 10th March 1956 and was burnt out.

The photographer has timed this shot perfectly to enable the world famous bridge across the river Severn to be prominent in the photograph. Yes, it is Ironbridge and this portrait of Stanier 3MT Class 2-6-2T No.40205 leaving Ironbridge and Broseley station with a southbound train was also taken on 1st April 1961. The sun seems to have burst through an otherwise overcast sky at just the right moment, proving that, just occasionally, the elements are sometimes kind to railway photographers. Curiously, the former GWR shed at Shrewsbury had three of these 2-6-2Ts on its books at the time of this photograph, the others being Nos.40086 and 40110, but all were transferred away later the same month.

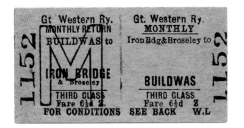

The history of the Wellington to Much Wenlock branch is complex because four different companies were involved in its construction. The section from Wellington (Ketley Junction) to Lightmoor, where it met the GWR line from Shifnal, was built by the Wellington & Severn Junction Railway and opened on 1st May 1857. The short stretch from Lightmoor to Coalbrookdale was already *in situ* having been laid as part of the GWR line from Madeley Junction (Shifnal) which opened on 1st June 1854. Railway expansion was also being planned for the opposite bank of the river Severn and in February 1862 the Severn Valley line was opened at the same time as the 3 miles-long branch from Much Wenlock, built by the Much Wenlock & Severn Junction Railway, the two lines meeting just across the river at Buildwas. Coalbrookdale was not linked with Buildwas until the Much Wenlock, Craven Arms and Coalbrookdale Railway, commonly known as the 'Wenlock Railway', opened its short link across the Albert Edward bridge on 1st November 1864. The last mentioned company was also responsible for the construction of the delightfully scenic stretch of line beyond Much Wenlock down to Craven Arms, but this was a very early casualty, closing to passengers on 31st December 1951. In this shot a Wellington to Much Wenlock train, hauled by Ivatt 2MT Class 2-6-2T No.41204, pauses at Coalbrookdale station on 1st April 1961. This area is widely regarded as being the cradle of the industrial revolution and as early as the sixteenth century coal was exported down the river Severn. The village of Ironbridge takes its name from a bridge, depicted in the previous illustration, made from components cast at Coalbrookdale in 1779.

After leaving Coalbrookdale station (seven miles from Wellington) the line crossed over the river Severn on the Albert Edward bridge and then ran parallel to the track of the Severn Valley line for a short distance. The Much Wenlock branch then diverged and climbed steeply to Buildwas station where the branch platform was on a much higher level than those serving Severn Valley line trains. In this illustration a train bound for Much Wenlock is seen at Buildwas on 30th August 1958. Much of the station area is now part of a power station complex.

Railway stations do not come much prettier than Much Wenlock, seen here in this picture which was taken on the same day as the previous shot. The station was brought into use on 1st February 1862 when the line to Buildwas was opened by the Much Wenlock & Severn Junction Railway. The section beyond here to Craven Arms was opened in stages by the Much Wenlock, Craven Arms & Coalbrookdale Railway, the first through services running on 16th December 1867. The latter company was absorbed by the GWR in 1896. Services between Much Wenlock and Craven Arms were, as previously stated, withdrawn from 31st December 1951. The link from Much Wenlock to Wellington remained but the service provided was poor, only seven weekday trains in each direction being advertised in the winter 1954/55 public timetable. This service was also deemed to be uneconomic and was withdrawn from 23rd July 1962.

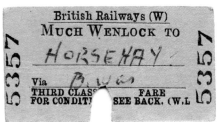

The railways in the Welsh valleys developed to serve the coal and steel industries and this shot, taken at Pontypridd on 28th September 1963, shows two coal trains in the station area, a very typical scene at that time. The train on the left is headed by 8750 Class 0-6-0PT No.9668, while that on the right has an unidentified 5600 Class 0-6-2T as motive power. The grey coloured wagons are unbraked while the wagons painted in bauxite are vacuum braked. The line through Pontypridd was part of the Taff Vale Railway from Cardiff to Abercynon which opened on 9th October 1840. This line was soon extended up the valley of the river Taff to Merthyr.

Towering mountains at the head of the Rhondda valley dominate the backdrop to this picture of a diesel multiple unit leaving Treherbert for Cardiff on 28th September 1963. In 1845 the trustees of the Marquis of Bute bought a farm for £11,000 with the intention of sinking a shaft for the first steam coal pit in the Rhondda valley. A trial pit was sunk in 1850 but progress was slow because equipment had to be carried over rough tracks from Dinas, then the terminus of the Taff Vale Railway from Pontypridd which had opened in 1841. Production began in early 1855 and during the following year an extension from Dinas was opened, it then becoming possible to transport coal by rail from Treherbert for the first time, thus giving the industry a tremendous boost. Passenger trains started running to and from Treherbert from 7th January 1863. The line continued beyond there through the Rhondda tunnel to Blaengwynfi and Bridgend/ Neath, the 3,443 yards-long tunnel, which opened in 1890, being the longest on the WR wholly within Wales. The train service westwards from Treherbert was replaced by buses in February 1968 when structural movement was detected in the tunnel and its 'temporary' closure became permanent, the bus service ceasing entirely from 14th December 1970 when the line was officially closed.

Maerdy station – at 900 feet above sea level it was the highest point on the Taff Vale Railway system. The Maerdy branch was developed in rather unusual circumstances, on a piecemeal basis, diverging from the Rhondda valley line at Porth and by 1856 had reached Ferndale. The final section became available for 'main line' through traffic when the Taff Vale Railway bought the private mineral line that linked Ferndale with Maerdy. Passenger trains did not commence operation along the entire line until about 1889. The line's primary purpose was to serve various collieries, especially the large pit at Maerdy, which opened in 1875, and by 1918 the colliery was reputed to employ more than 2,000 men. The mine was closed in 1940 as a result of the suspension of coal exports but was totally rebuilt in 1949 due to its vast coal reserves and subsequently survived to become the last productive mine in the Rhondda, closing in 1986. The site was cleared in 1990 and is now occupied by a factory. Railway enthusiasts remember Maerdy colliery because an ex-GWR pannier tank locomotive, No. 9792, was employed there on shunting duties after BR steam had finished. In this picture, taken on 29th September 1962, a d.m.u. is seen waiting to leave for Porth; the track on the left leads to the colliery.

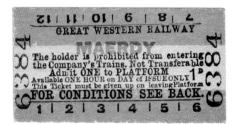

Photographed against a background of man-made mountains of pit waste, Quaker's Yard (Low Level) station is seen in this illustration, with a diesel multiple unit, presumably bound for Cardiff, negotiating the tight curve into the platform on 28th September 1963. This line was brought into use on 12th April 1841 when the Taff Vale Railway opened its extension from Abercynon to Merthyr. At the time of this photograph the station still exuded plenty of Great Western atmosphere, with the distinctive waiting hut (note the unsightly chimney!), lower quadrant signals and gas lamps. The large running-in board on the up platform doubtless advised passengers to change for the High Level station which was served by trains between Pontypool Road and Neath. Quaker's Yard was named after a nearby burial ground of the Society of Friends.

The first railway to reach Merthyr was the Taff Vale Railway which opened its Plymouth Street station on 12th April 1841 at a time when Merthyr was booming as a result of the rapidly expanding coal and iron industries. The Merthyr extension of the Vale of Neath Railway opened its station at the High Street on 2nd November 1853, the Taff Vale transferring its passenger trains to that station on 1st August 1877, and Merthyr High Street eventually became the passenger terminus for all railways that served the town. In 1914 the station was, remarkably, served by five different companies and more than fifty weekday departures were scheduled, including through services to Newport and a daily express train to Swansea via Hirwaun. The station then comprised five platforms under a timber roof, the main part of which was designed by Brunel and lasted until 1953. In this picture, taken on 4th November 1961, there is plenty of activity as the crew of locomotive No.6433 attempt to refill its pannier tanks, a ritual that was an everyday sight at stations with watering facilities in steam days.

Pannier tank locomotive No.6433, which is seen in the previous picture, sits out in the winter sunshine at Merthyr High Street on 4th November 1961 prior to departing with a local train to Pontsticill Junction, where connections were made with trains to and from Brecon. The principal service from South Wales to Brecon was from Newport via Bargoed and Dowlais which by-passed Merthyr, so an infrequent connecting service was provided. By the date of this photograph there were only two departures each weekday, so the service was very sparse indeed. There were only three passenger lines radiating from Merthyr by this time, the busiest route being the line to Cardiff, while a service ran to Hirwaun where it connected with trains to Neath and Swansea.

A Stephenson Locomotive Society (Midland Area) rail tour, hauled/propelled by GWR 6400 Class 0-6-0 pannier tank No.6416, is seen at Nantymoel on 2nd July 1960. This fascinating tour, which started at Bridgend, traversed some of the more obscure branches in the Welsh valleys, including those to Blaengarw, Nantymoel and the fiercely-graded Glyncorrwg branch. The first branch visited was the line to Blaengarw and after that the train made its way to Nantymoel, where it is pictured waiting in the rather dilapidated former station against a backdrop of distant mountains. The seven miles-long standard gauge branch from Tondu to Nantymoel was opened by the Ogmore Valley Railway on 1st August 1865 and, by virtue of running powers over the Llynvi Railway Company's tracks, was able to run mineral trains right through to Porthcawl Harbour. Latterly, the branch had a poor service of around half a dozen trains on weekdays only, so it probably came as no surprise to local people when the service between Tondu and Nantymoel was withdrawn from 5th May 1958. The paper stickers in the cab of the auto coach indicate the train's reporting number which would have been advised to operating staff when the timings were published.

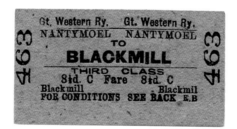

The Stephenson Locomotive Society rail tour, which is seen in the previous picture, is depicted at Cymmer West junction. After its journey up the Nantymoel line the participants were treated to a trip along the South Wales Mineral Railway's Glyncorrwg branch as far as North Rhondda halt. This line, which was opened to Glyncorrwg in March 1863 to serve various collieries, was originally broad gauge but was converted to standard gauge in May 1872. The line was taken over by the GWR in December 1907. Participants on the rail tour were obliged to change trains at Caerau, where they boarded vintage vehicles owned by the National Coal Board that were normally used to convey miners from Cymmer Corrwg to North Rhondda Halt. Motive power for this part of the tour was 8750 Class 0-6-0PT No.9634. One can only imagine what a thrilling experience the journey from Caerau to North Rhondda must have been as the pannier tank locomotive blasted its way through the narrow defile of Glyn Corrwg, propelling its three coaches up unbelievable gradients of 1 in 28/22. A public passenger service operated up the valley from 28th March 1918 to 22nd September 1930 but, of course, the miners' trains continued long after that date. The train is seen here on its way back from North Rhondda Halt, with No.9634 being apparently none the worse for its exertions! The train has just crossed over the Rhondda & Swansea Bay Railway on an overbridge (note the telegraph pole above the hut) and is approaching the junction with the branch from Abergwynfi which is coming in on the right of the shot.

The station running-in board clearly identifies the location of this picture which was taken looking northwards on the bright morning of 4th November 1961. Pontsticill Junction was on the Newport to Brecon line which had an infrequent service consisting of only three through trains each way on Mondays to Fridays, while four trains operated on Saturdays. Certain sections of the line were, however, served by trains on other routes and had a somewhat more frequent service. Most trains took about 2½ hours to cover the 47 miles between the two towns. The train in the platform appears to be an auto train working to Merthyr, a service that was provided, as previously mentioned, to connect with trains to Brecon. This service was withdrawn from 13th November 1961, just over a week after this photograph was taken. The station here was in a very tranquil location, surrounded by mountains and situated above a reservoir which is visible on the left – a far cry indeed from the heavy industry of Merthyr only a few miles distant. The peace and quiet was rudely shattered every so often, however, when a train approached

from Merthyr up the tortuous 1 in 45/50 incline which applied most of the way, and trains completely reversed direction during the 6¾ miles-long journey. The hills here still echo to the sound of steam, but these days it is the more subdued noise of a narrow gauge locomotive chuffing along on the Brecon Mountain Railway rather than the urgent bark of a pannier tank engine displaying its raw power on the climb from Merthyr.

In the nineteenth century the towns of Merthyr and Dowlais were reputed to constitute the largest group of ironworks in the world and the works at Dowlais alone was reckoned to employ 5,000 people at one time. In this picture GWR 5600 class 0-6-2T No.5652 is depicted shunting at Dowlais (Cae Harris) station on 4th November 1961, presumably after arrival off the Taff Bargoed Joint Railway with a passenger train from Nelson & Llancaiach, this line being a joint venture by the GWR and Rhymney Railway. It opened in 1876, its main purpose being the movement of iron ore from the docks at Cardiff to the hungry furnaces at Dowlais. There was a daunting seven miles-long climb at gradients of 1 in 40/49 but, even so, in 1913 the Rhymney Railway is reckoned to have hauled 400,000 tons up to Dowlais. Note the huge slag heaps in the background, their varying size and weird shapes being reminiscent of the surface of the moon! There were three other stations in Dowlais, perhaps the best known being Dowlais Top, on the Newport to Brecon line, while High Street was served by trains running between Merthyr and Abergavenny.

Crumlin viaduct was undoubtedly one of the truly great engineering achievements of the railway age in South Wales. It was built as part of the Newport, Abergavenny & Hereford Railway's (NA&HR) Taff Vale extension and took the Pontypool Road to Quaker's Yard line across the river Ebbw. Construction commenced in 1853 and within two years the piers had been raised and the abutments were ready. The viaduct consisted of ten spans, each 150ft wide from pier to pier, and the maximum height of the structure above the river bed was 208ft. The viaduct was 1,658 feet-long and a total of 2,550 tons of iron were used in its construction; the cost of the works amounted to £62,000. At the time it was built it was reputed to be the third highest structure of its kind in the world. In May 1857 it was ready for testing and six locomotives, apparently loaded with lead and weighing 380 tons, were paraded across the viaduct watched by a crowd of 20,000 onlookers. The structure was formally opened on 1st June 1857, an arch of flowers and evergreens apparently being constructed on the viaduct for the ceremony. In 1928 the viaduct was re-decked by the GWR and during this work single line working was instituted and was later made permanent by gauntletting the two tracks to avoid two trains crossing. The NA&HR later became part of the GWR which extended the line as far as Middle Duffryn Junction with a connection to the Vale of Neath Railway. The distance from Pontypool Road to Middle Duffryn Junction was 20¼ miles and, remarkably, there were no fewer than ten junctions with other lines, thus providing the NA&HR and its successors with a trunk route striking into the heart of the South Wales coalfield, and many millions of tons of coal doubtless passed over the line during the ensuing years. Towards the end, there were only five weekday passenger trains each way over the entire length of the Neath to Pontypool Road route, though some intermediate sections had a more frequent service, and the line was closed to passenger traffic on 15th June 1964. The viaduct was demolished with almost indecent haste during the following year and this very impressive monument to railway engineering was soon no more. In this superb vista, an industrial haze masks the bottom of the Ebbw valley as a train from Pontypool Road, almost lost in the distance, crosses the viaduct on 31st October 1959. Crumlin (High Level) station just appears at the bottom of the picture.

The line between Whitland and Cardigan was built to serve the important slate quarries at Glogue and opened in three distinct sections. The first stretch, from the main line junction 2¼ miles beyond Whitland, to Llanfyrnach, was opened by the Whitland & Taf Vale Railway Company on 24th March 1873. The river Taf rises in the Mynydd Precelli, near Glogue, and should not be confused with the more widely known river in Glamorganshire. The next section to be brought into use was the short 3¾ miles-long stretch onward to Crymmych Arms and this opened in October of the following year. The company decided to press on to Cardigan and in 1877 obtained powers to construct the eleven miles-long section from Crymmych Arms, this opening on 1st September 1886. The GWR took over operation of the entire line from this date and absorbed the local company in 1890. The 27¾ miles-long line, which was built as a light railway, was extremely picturesque and followed the course of the river Taf for some distance. There were tight curves and very steep gradients, such as the 1 in 35 up to the summit at Cymmych Arms, and other inclines were only slightly less severe. The route ran through a very thinly populated rural area and, latterly, the passenger service, for which one-coach trains normally sufficed, generally consisted of three up and four down trains on weekdays only. The inevitable closure came on 10th September 1962 while the goods service lasted until 25th May 1963, from which date this attractive byway was closed completely. Here, a Cardigan to Whitland train is seen taking water at Glogue on 4th August 1962.

Crymmych Arms station served only a small settlement and here a southbound train pauses to collect a few passengers and a dog! Despite the meagre amount of traffic generated by this station it was equipped with a commodious signal box and a very large running-in board. Note that there are some wagons in the goods yard behind the fence. What a wonderful cloud formation! This shot was also taken on 4th August 1962.

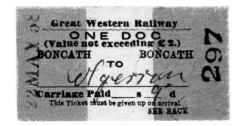

There were no significant intermediate centres of population between Whitland and Cardigan and this picture bears testament to the totally unremunerative nature of the branch and the scattered communities it served. A rather travel-stained GWR 4500 2-6-2T No.4569 stands at Boncath station with (what appears to be) the 6.20am Whitland to Cardigan train on an August morning in 1962. Boncath was exactly 21 miles from Whitland and this train was booked to leave there at 7.55am, so it must have been one of the slowest in Great Britain. Travelling on this lovely line must have been a memorable experience for railway aficionados, but one dreads to think what *bona fide* passengers made of it all!

Cardigan station – a true outpost of the Western Region. The Whitland to Cardigan branch had little traffic potential and even way back in 1953, in the days when the private car was the preserve of the better off, the branch had a very poor, and extremely slow, service. In this shot, which also dates from August 1962, an unidentified 4575 Class 2-6-2T shunts the goods yard while the branch passenger train sits in the platform, apparently with another engine of the same class in charge. A rare, relatively busy scene at Cardigan station.

Confusion at Cardigan! There was clearly a lack of co-ordination between the various organisations responsible for street signs in Cardigan and this fine display of vintage signage was photographed at the end of the station road in August 1962. One wonders if any drivers conveying intending train passengers were so bamboozled by the signs they simply turned around and drove to Whitland instead. Happy motoring!

The 10.00am departure to Whitland is depicted simmering in Cardigan station on a sunny August morning in 1962; the train engine is, once again, GWR 2-6-2T 4500 Class No.4569 which was nominally allocated to Neyland shed but, in reality, probably spent a week at a time away from its home depot stabled at Whitland and Cardigan where there were sub-sheds. Any prospective passengers would doubtless have provided themselves with sustenance for the journey, the scheduled arrival time at Whitland being 11.40am. By the time of this picture the writing was already on the wall for this charming backwater and weeds have already started to take a hold on the platform and in the goods yard.

Fishguard and Neyland – a tale of two ports. The broad gauge line of the South Wales Railway (SWR) had reached Carmarthen by 1852 and it was envisaged that the line's western terminus would be sited at Fishguard, with a branch to Haverfordwest. There was a sudden change of plan, however, and it was decided to extend the line to the shore of Milford Haven at Neyland Point, apparently because Brunel favoured Neyland which had a sheltered, deep water anchorage. The GWR operated traffic over the SWR and the two companies amalgamated in 1863. Consequently, Neyland, which was known at various times as New Milford and Milford Haven, became the GWR's port for Ireland, opening in April 1856. The town immediately grew in size and the regular steamship service to Waterford, plus other sailings, transformed its fortunes. Meanwhile, the North Pembrokeshire & Fishguard Railway's efforts to reach Fishguard came to nothing, but in 1898 this company was bought by the GWR who in the following year extended the existing line from Clynderwen to Letterston via Rosebush on to Goodwick. In 1906 the half-mile gap from Goodwick to Fishguard Harbour was bridged and the 10¾ miles-long stretch from Clarbeston Road to Letterston was completed, thus providing a main line route to London. The Rosebush line was beset with sharp curves plus heavy gradients and was unsuitable for main line traffic. The construction of port facilities at Fishguard Harbour involved the blasting of rock to create a 27-acre site and the first sailing left for Ireland on 30th August 1906. The boat trains from Paddington were transferred to the new route and Neyland lapsed into relative obscurity, the branch eventually being closed to passengers from 15th June 1964. In this picture 8750 Class 0-6-0PT No.8739 is seen awaiting departure from Fishguard Harbour with a local train on 4th August 1962. Note that the two coaches are in different liveries, the leading coach is in carmine and cream while the other one is in (what is commonly known as) chocolate and cream.

Of all the attractive country branches featured in this album, the 60 miles-long Mid Wales line from Moat Lane Junction to Brecon was perhaps the most appealing. This route encapsulated all of the charm of a quiet rural line, including glorious river scenery, well-kept stations, an unhurried, relaxed atmosphere and slow schedules which gave passengers plenty of time to view the passing scene from the carriage window. From Moat Lane to Llanidloes the line followed the river Severn and then the narrow valley of the river Dulas, steadily climbing up to a summit 947ft above sea level at Pant-y-dwr, which later became the highest point on the Cambrian Railway's system. The line then ran alongside the river Marteg, a tributary of the river Wye, before entering the valley of the infant waters of the river Wye above Rhayader. The railway then followed the river for mile after beautiful mile until Three Cocks Junction was reached, where it joined the line from Hereford. The final entry into Brecon was within sight of the river Usk – could the promoters have built a more scenic railway? The route was constructed in two distinct sections, the first, from Moat Lane Junction to Llanidloes, built by the Llanidloes & Newtown Railway, opened for goods traffic on 31st August 1859 while passenger trains started running on 2nd September. The Mid Wales Railway was responsible for the other, and far longer, part of the route southwards from Llanidloes to Brecon which opened for goods traffic on 1st September 1864 and for passenger workings on 21st September. It should be mentioned that, strictly speaking, only the section south of Llanidloes should be referred to as the Mid Wales line. Here, on a very frosty 22nd December 1962, a rather dirty Ivatt-designed Class 2MT 2-6-0 waits to leave Moat Lane with the 9.55am to Brecon, where the train terminated at 12.35pm.

There was still frost on the sleepers and surrounding fields when the 12.35pm Aberystwyth to Crewe/Shrewsbury halted at Moat Lane Junction on 22nd December 1962; the train engine is a GWR 'Manor' Class 4-6-0 but the pilot locomotive cannot be identified. Double-headed trains were an everyday sight on this line, which was very heavily graded, the toughest climb being the 3½ miles-long ascent at 1 in 52/56 from Llanbrynmair to Talerddig summit. The locomotive on the left which is partially visible is an Ivatt Class 2MT 2-6-0 resting between duties on the Mid Wales line, the tracks of which pass behind the signal box on the right. It may seem strange that the 'main line' platforms here were on a curve and the much less important Mid Wales platform was straight, but it has to be borne in mind that the first line to be constructed was the route towards Brecon, the Newtown & Machynlleth line not opening until 1863, four years after the section to Llanidloes.

G.W.R.

Moat Lane

Moat Lane Junction again, but this time looking north-westwards towards Caersws and Machynlleth. In this scene, recorded on 9th September 1960, Ivatt Class 2MT 2-6-0 No.46519 simmers in the up loop platform with the stock of a Mid Wales line train while another locomotive of the same class moves around the station area in the background. In November 1960 Oswestry shed had an allocation of no fewer than 22 of these relatively modern 'Moguls' for use on Mid Wales line and other services, and it is likely that the engines spent long periods away from their home shed, receiving routine servicing at Brecon, and also Llanidloes and Moat Lane, both of which were sub-sheds of Oswestry. The large running-in board on the platform was a classic and exhorted passengers to 'Change for Llanidloes, Rhayader, Builth Wells, Brecon and South Wales'. It seems likely, however, that only the most patient and philosophical traveller would have wished to use the Brecon train to reach south Wales because (in the summer 1962 timetable) there were only two through trains, timetabled on weekdays only, and the journey time was an extremely leisurely 2 hours 45 minutes, but the landscape through which the trains traversed was in a class of its own. Then there was the problem of getting from Brecon to one's destination!

The tiny station of Dolwen Halt, between Moat Lane Junction and Llanidloes, is depicted here with a tender-first Ivatt Class 2MT 'Mogul' running in with the 12.27pm Moat Lane Junction to Llanidloes local working on 22nd December 1962. The impressive mountains in the distance give an idea of the outstanding scenery traversed by the line. The two through trains each weekday were supplemented by various short workings, for example there were five services each way between Llanidloes and Moat Lane Junction, one daily train in each direction being provided mainly for school children. A few trains started or finished their journeys at Builth Road, where the Mid Wales line passed underneath the Central Wales line, and there was an evening train from Builth Road to Builth Wells that connected with the last train of the day via the Central Wales line from Shrewsbury.

You can almost feel the penetrating cold as Ivatt Class 2MT No.46518, shrouded in steam, pulls out of Llanidloes with a train to Brecon in December 1962 while a train heading in the opposite direction waits in the loop platform. The closure of this delightful country line had already been announced when this shot was taken and many of the staff had probably lost heart, hence the filthy condition of the locomotive in this picture. The imposing building on the left is the former headquarters of the Llanidloes & Newtown Railway. Note the ticket collector's hut at the top of the footbridge steps and various designs of ornate gas lamp.

G.W.R.

Llanidloes

THE MID WALES LINE

There are a few diehard passengers in this picture of the 12.45pm Builth Wells to Moat Lane Junction train awaiting departure from Llanidloes, also on 22nd December 1962. This shot was taken from the steps of the footbridge and gives a reasonably panoramic view of the station and its environs, despite the gas lamp which is in a rather intrusive position. Llanidloes was to some degree the operational hub of the Moat Lane Junction to Brecon line and boasted a two-road engine shed which can be discerned in the background of this photograph. The shed was, as previously mentioned, a sub shed of Oswestry and dated from the opening of the line from Newtown in 1859. It was a very sad event when the line was closed at the end of 1962, an event that was keenly felt in Llanidloes where forty members of BR staff were made redundant. In more prosperous times gone by the station's facilities were very busy with special trains organised for the conveyance of livestock in connection with Llanidloes fair. A point of interest to railway historians was Pentpontbren Junction, south of here, where the track of the ill-fated Manchester & Milford Railway joined from Llangurig; no scheduled train ever ran over this section, the line being lifted in 1882.

The tracks of the Mid Wales Railway went as far as Talyllyn Junction, the section beyond that point to Brecon having been opened by the Brecon & Merthyr Railway (B&M) on 1st May 1863. Talyllyn Junction station (610 feet above sea level) is seen in this picture which was taken on 14th May 1962; the tracks to the left are for Llanidloes and Hereford while those going off to the right are those of the B&M to Merthyr. Note the characteristic 'pagoda' waiting shelter on the far platform. The Mid Wales Railway originally had its own station just to the north of this spot, this being in addition to the B&M premises; the station lasted until 1878. There was a triangle here and this enabled trains from the Mid Wales line to run direct to south Wales. Despite its lack of traffic potential, the Mid Wales Railway had its high spots, one undoubtedly being in the 1870s when express services were run from Aberystwyth/Moat Lane Junction to Brecon, and another heyday was during the First World War when heavy coal trains from south Wales ran to Scotland for the Grand Fleet. When BR's deficit increased it was inevitable that lightly trafficked lines would come under scrutiny, and the Moat Lane to Talyllyn Junction line was included in a closure proposal for all of the branch lines that radiated from Brecon, the public inquiry taking place in early 1962. Indeed, this line was cited to be the heaviest loss-maker, and BR stated that the service was losing £150,000 per annum and that almost £200,000 was needed for track repairs during the ensuing five years. Closure was sanctioned from 31st December 1962, the last public trains running on 29th December, and it is recorded that the 5.05pm Brecon to Moat Lane train, powered by Ivatt Class 2MT No.46518, was the last through working in the northbound direction, while the last Mid Wales line departure of all from Brecon was the 9.35pm SO to Builth Wells, hauled by No.46526. The following day a ten-coach Stephenson Locomotive Society special, worked by a brace of Ivatt 2-6-0s, traversed the route after which one of the best-loved lines in Wales disappeared from the railway map for ever.

When the Oswestry & Newtown Railway (O&NR) opened as far as Pool Quay on 1st May 1860 the people of Llanfyllin saw the chance of a rail connection to Oswestry and lodged a bill in Parliament for an independent branch which was intended to connect with the O&NR at Llanymynech. In the event their bill failed and the branch to Llanfyllin was authorised by the O&NR Act of 17th May 1861. The 8½ miles-long branch followed the course of the river Cain and the initial three miles-long section as far as Llansantffraid, the only original intermediate station, was built as a double track formation, but only one line was laid. The rest of the branch was constructed as a single track line. Services commenced on 10th April 1863, trains running through to Oswestry. In 1866 more intermediate stations were opened, at Llanfechain and Bryngwyn. Latterly, traffic on the branch was light, the winter 1953/54 timetable advertising a service of just five weekdays only trains. Goods traffic ceased in 1964 and the end for this obscure branch came on 18th January 1965 when the passenger service succumbed, the Whitchurch to Welshpool service being withdrawn at the same time. This is a June 1962 picture.

A view taken at the south end of Oswestry station, in June 1962, showing a rather dirty 4300 Class 'Mogul' No.7313 taking water while working a train to Welshpool. The route towards Welshpool was brought into use as far as Pool Quay on 1st May 1860 and the remaining section on to Welshpool was opened on 14th August 1860. The line from Ellesmere opened, as previously stated, on 27th July 1864. The summer 1962 public timetable reveals that the Whitchurch to Welshpool line had a poor local service of around eight trains each way on weekdays but these were bolstered by a number of holiday trains on summer Saturdays; the service lasted until 18th January 1965. In times past Oswestry was an important railway centre, being located on the main goods artery from south Wales to Merseyside and also on the route from the Welsh coast to centres in the north of England. The town became the nerve centre of the Cambrian Railway's operations and, in addition to the six-road engine shed, a locomotive repair works was constructed plus carriage and wagon shops. Trains to and from Blodwell quarry continued to pass through the closed station until 1988.

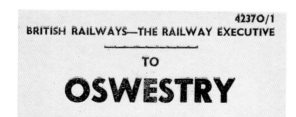

The first railway line to reach Oswestry was the short 2½ miles-long branch from Gobowen, which opened on 23rd December 1848, and in this illustration GWR 6400 Class 0-6-0PT No.6403 is seen waiting in the bay platform at the north end of Oswestry station in June 1962 with a Gobowen train. Trains on this line originally ran into a separate station in the town, but this was closed in July 1924 and services diverted to the former Cambrian Railway station (seen here) which had been enlarged by the GWR. Note that the train comprises one non-corridor suburban coach and a main line corridor vehicle. A shuttle service operated between Oswestry and Gobowen, where connections were made with trains on the main line from Chester to Shrewsbury, and in the mid-1950s the public timetable listed almost two dozen trains between the two stations. The principal station building, seen in the background, was formerly the headquarters of the Cambrian Railway and still survives at the time of writing.

In the 1870s the Cambrian Railway was considering an independent route for mineral traffic from the south Wales coalfield to Merseyside but two links were missing, Connah's Quay to Bidston and Wrexham to Ellesmere. There was also a need for a more direct route from Whitchurch and Ellesmere to Wrexham instead of the roundabout journey which involved changing trains at Whittington. On 31st July 1885 the Wrexham & Ellesmere Railway (W&ER) obtained an Act for the construction of the 12¾ miles-long line between the towns but the scheme was beset with difficulties – the first sod was not cut until 11th July 1892 – and opening was severely delayed. The great day finally came, however, and the single track route was eventually declared open on 2nd November 1895. There were originally three intermediate stations, all of which had passing loops, and in later years a further six halts were built, giving a total of nine stations between Wrexham and Ellesmere. Wrexham Central station is

seen in this illustration, looking eastwards in June 1962, with an auto-train for Ellesmere occupying one of the platforms; note the clerestory coach on the right. The premises seen here were opened by the Wrexham, Mold & Connah's Quay Railway on 1st November 1887 and the W&ER made an end-on junction with this line. The rather unprepossessing station buildings were supposed to be 'temporary' structures when built in 1887 but were still doing yeoman service more than seventy years later! A new station, built on a different site in 1998, replaced the premises seen here.

Great expectations. When the Wrexham to Ellesmere line was constructed, judging by the length of the platforms, the promoters obviously had hopes that Bangor-on-Dee would be served by quite long trains and the single-coach auto-train seen in this June 1962 picture looks rather lost and insignificant standing at such a long platform. The line was considered for closure way back in the early 1950s, but nothing materialised until almost ten years later when the future of the line was severely jeopardised by bridge repairs, estimated to cost £80,000, and the annual operating loss of £26,000 per annum. The bridge repairs probably tipped the balance in favour of closure and the line carried its last passengers on 8th September 1962, the official closure date being Monday 10th September. Goods trains continued to run along short sections for some time afterwards, the thrice weekly Whitchurch to Ellesmere service lasting until 27th March 1965.

Ellesmere station on a June day in 1962 and former GWR Class 1400 0-4-2T No.1458, of Oswestry shed, has just arrived with an auto-train working from Wrexham. Note the lady pushing the vintage push chair – how comfortable the baby looks! Ellesmere was located on the Oswestry to Whitchurch secondary line, a route proposed by the Oswestry, Ellesmere & Whitchurch Railway; the line received the Royal Assent on 1st August 1861 and the single track route between Whitchurch and Ellesmere opened for passenger business on 4th May 1863. A notable feature of this line was the crossing of Fenn's Moss by means of a timber-framed brushwood raft. The remaining 7¼ miles-long stretch on to Oswestry was brought into use on 27th July 1864. The summer 1962 timetable listed eight return workings on the Wrexham to Ellesmere line on weekdays only and this proved to be the last public timetable in which the route appeared. Ellesmere lost its passenger service from 18th January 1965 when the Oswestry to Whitchurch service was withdrawn.

5	2nd-PRIVILEGE RETURN	PRIVILEGE-2nd RETURN	5
4	ELLESMERE to WREXHAM CENT.	Wrexham Cent to ELLESMERE	4
3	(W) Fare 1/4½ For conditions see over	Fare 1/4½ (W) For conditions see over	3

The 54 miles-long railway that links Dovey Junction with Pwllheli – known today as the Cambrian Coast Line – is undoubtedly one of the most scenic lines featured in this album. Hemmed in by the natural obstacles of the sea and the Cambrian mountains, the line offers one of the most relaxing and enjoyable journeys one could wish for. The line opened throughout on 10th October 1867 but this bland statement conceals the fact that the route was largely brought into operation on a piecemeal basis over a number of years. The Aberystwyth & Welsh Coast Railway (A&WCR) obtained an Act to build the line on 22nd July 1861 and the 12¼ miles-long Machynlleth to Borth stretch was the first section opened, the opening date being 1st July 1863. The Borth to Aberystwyth portion was brought into use on 23rd June 1864 and completion of the Oswestry, Ellesmere & Whitchurch Railway's line a few weeks later ensured that through services from Whitchurch to the Welsh resort began almost immediately. The A&WCR wanted to secure a quick return on their investment and the opening of the line from Whitchurch, not to mention the through coaches from Euston, certainly achieved this objective. Dovey Junction station, where the down 'Cambrian Coast Express' is seen pausing in July 1962, is located on windswept marshland and was built purely as an interchange point between the Aberystwyth and Pwllheli routes, and does not have any road access. The locomotive depicted is GWR-designed 'Manor' 4-6-0 No.7823 *Hook Norton Manor* which actually was constructed in the BR era, emerging from Swindon Works in December 1950.

Aberdovey is the first station of any note after leaving Dovey Junction on the Pwllheli line and the station is seen here, looking southwards, in July 1962. The section from here to Llwyngwril, opened on 24th October 1863, was one of those brought into use before through traffic commenced running on the Dovey Junction to Pwllheli line. The line took a sinuous course around the back of the town to avoid the harbour and this necessitated the construction of four tunnels in addition to other heavy earthworks. The ornate up platform canopy (on the left) was dismantled in October 1980 by members of the Bala Lake Railway for further use at Llanuwchllyn. It is thought that the canopy previously stood at the old Pwllheli station before the line was extended to the present station's location in 1909.

A novice fireman? The smoke effect being emitted by 4300 Class 2-6-0 No.6375 darkens the sky over Aberdovey station as the locomotive pulls out with a train to Machyllneth in July 1962. The engine's very dirty condition will be noted – obviously Croes Newydd shed, where the locomotive was allocated, was short of cleaners. One wonders how long the rather fine starting signal with a wooden post had been standing at that spot; perhaps its history could be traced back to the line's earliest days.

Towyn – home of the world famous Tal-y-Llyn Railway. Judging by the puddles on the platforms there had been some recent rain, but the weather seems to be a little brighter as *ex*-GWR 'Mogul' No.6375 slows to a halt at Towyn station, presumably with the train depicted in the previous photograph. Note that at that time the station boasted a parcels office and cloak room. The section from Aberdovey to Llwyngwril, through Towyn, was one of the easier stretches of the Dovey Junction to Pwllheli line to be constructed because it traversed relatively flat terrain; the line was brought into use on 24th October 1863 with three trains daily each way.

The 'Morfa Mawddach' sign on the running-in board, seen in this July 1962 picture, seems to be in pristine condition and unaffected by the corrosive sea air that abounds in these parts. This is explained by the fact that the station was formerly known as Barmouth Junction and it had been renamed from the commencement of the 1960 summer timetable on 13th June. Apparently the renaming caused a spot of confusion amongst passengers because the station nameboards were not changed immediately and still displayed the old name a month later. In this illustration an *ex*-GWR 'Manor' Class 4-6-0 has just taken the line to Llangollen and Ruabon with an unidentified four-coach working. The station here was formerly

a triangular junction and opened to passengers on 3rd June 1867. The routes converging on Morfa Mawddach were single track lines, but both the Cambrian Coast line and the route from Ruabon had passing loops in the station thus giving rise to the double line junction seen here. The double track section was short, however, the lines merging into a single track before the viaduct was reached. In steam days this must have been a splendid spot at which to observe train movements, especially on a busy summer Saturday when packed trains of holiday-makers ensured that the lines were worked at almost maximum capacity. Traffic density on the Cambrian main line meant that some expresses from Paddington to the Welsh coast were routed via Ruabon and in the 1962 timetable the 9.00am Paddington to Pwllheli was advertised as conveying a restaurant car. This train left Ruabon at 1.13pm so passengers taking lunch at that time may have been distracted and missed some of the glorious scenery during the two-hour long journey to Morfa Mawddach.

The mountains of Snowdonia loom in the distance as BR Standard Class 4MT 4-6-0 No.75020 runs into Talsarnau with a southbound working in July 1962. This station, which serves only a small hamlet, is located about four miles north of Harlech. Rather alarmingly, it would appear that elementary signalling and safety rules have been completely disregarded but the signals controlled by the ground frame on the station had been 'pulled off' for both directions, thus permitting the frame to be 'switched out'. Note the wonderful cloud formation which adds so much interest to the scene.

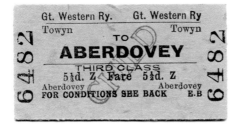

Once again the mountains of Snowdonia are visible as an unidentified BR Standard Class 4MT 4-6-0 hauling a southbound train negotiates the tight curve into Minffordd station in July 1962. The overbridge, which carries the narrow gauge Ffestiniog Railway (FR) across the tracks of the Cambrian Coast line, provides a perfect 'frame' for the picture. There are no signals or signal wires visible in this shot, so it is possible that by the time of this picture the signal box had been reduced in status to a ground frame, merely controlling access to the track on the left which led to the exchange sidings with the FR. Judging by the shiny rail surfaces the line to those sidings certainly seems to have been in regular use: perhaps the FR received regular wagonloads of coal. Note the vintage oil lamp standards which are very decorative, but one wonders what arrangements BR had in place for tending the lamps and ensuring they were lit (and extinguished!) at the appropriate times. In reality that was no problem, because the station was still staffed at that time.